AF576844

OLD CHINESE SNUFF BOTTLES

JADE

See Pages 10 to 15, & 92.

OLD CHINESE SNUFF BOTTLES

Notes, with a Catalogue of a Modest Collection

by Henry C. Hitt

Charles E. Tuttle Company
Rutland, Vermont & Tokyo, Japan

Representatives
Continental Europe: BOXERBOOKS, INC., ZURICH
British Isles: PRENTICE-HALL INTERNATIONAL, INC., London
Canada: HURTIG PUBLISHERS, Edmonton
Australasia: BOOK WISE (AUSTRALIA) PTY. LTD.
104-108 Sussex Street, Sydney 2000

Published by the Charles E. Tuttle Company, Inc.
of Rutland, Vermont & Tokyo, Japan
with editorial offices at
Suido 1-chome, 2-6, Bunkyo-ku, Tokyo, Japan

Libary of Congress Catalog Card No. 76-44088

International Standard Book No. 0-8048-1220-9

Second edition published privately by
Henry C. Hitt, Bremerton, Washington, 1945
First Tuttle edition, 1978

Printed in Japan

CONTENTS

PREFACE TO THE NEW EDITION

Among collectors of Chinese snuff bottles, the name of the late Henry C. Hitt has long commanded respect, not only as that of an ardent fellow collector but also as that of the author of the first book on the subject in any language—a work that had the great value of arousing collectors everywhere, even in China. This book, which appeared in first and second editions (the latter considerably enlarged) and was followed by a supplement, has in itself become a collector's item. Until now, however, it has been practically impossible to obtain in either of its editions, for it was a handmade book produced by lithographic methods, and it had little hope of ever being reprinted. The present edition remedies this lack by bringing together, in photographic reduction, facsimile copies of the expanded second edition (1945) and the supplement and thereby making available to a much wider audience Mr. Hitt's invaluable contribution to the fascinating subject of snuff-bottle collecting.

In his introduction to the second edition, Mr. Hitt wrote: "There is almost a total lack of literature on Chinese snuff bottles. This is, as far as is known, the only book on the subject, and there have been only a few magazine articles." To be sure, since the appearance of his book in 1945 there have been numerous other books and articles on the subject, but this by no means diminishes the value of his pioneering work or the honor he achieved by being one of the first to share his knowledge with other enthusiastic collectors. It is therefore a pleasure for the publisher to bring his revealing and altogether charming book into print once again and thus to perform a service for the now greatly increased number of collectors.

PREFACE

The first edition of this first book on Chinese snuff bottle collecting was so enthusiastically received by both the museums and collectors, and generated so much new material and constructive criticism, and such a demand for more copies, that a new and enlarged second edition seems necessary without waiting for war conditions to permit publication through usual channels. So again I present a hand made book, produced by photographic* methods.

The new binding is copied from an old Chinese book, though you need not read this our book from the back forward, as is the Chinese way. The text is largely new or rewritten, and descriptions and sketches of a dozen or so new, and very interesting, bottles have been added. About as many others have been deleted as not particularly contributing to the book's contents. An index and a bibliography are important additions.

In this form the book is still an interim edition and it is hoped, and expected, that it will bring much welcome correspondence, numerous corrections and criticisms and additional new material to be incorporated in a later printed or lithographed* edition. Until then it will necessarily have to be an extremely limited hand made product.

My rich reward for a lot of exacting work will come in new friends and new finds of bottles and data. They will be welcome, both friends and finds.

Many have helped build this little book but I will restrict my public thanks to the most indefatigable of all, my good friend H. Sooysmith, collector and dealer of Portland, Oregon.

BREMERTON, WASH, U.S.A.
JANUARY, 1945

* LITHOGRAPHED
SER. #29 AND UP.
JULY 1945.

Henry C. Fritt

ONE HUNDRED AND FORTY FIVE YEARS AGO a collection of 2390 Chinese snuff bottles of topaz, carnelian, amber, and jade was dug up where they had been hidden in a garden outside the walls of Peking.

They were a part of the treasure of HO-SHÊN, the last great Grand Secretary of State of Emperor CHIEN LUNG (1735-1796).

HO-SHÊN was a man of great ability, sound judgement, and real devotion to CH'IEN LUNG and the greatest era of China's history, but he accumulated such power and such a vast fortune that within a week of the death of CH'IEN LUNG in 1799 the new Emperor CH'IA CHING (Ch'ien Lung's 15th son) preferred charges against HO-SHÊN. Under torture he disclosed the hiding place of his treasure, including his snuff bottle collection.

The official inventory of his gold bars silver, jewels, jades, brocades, furs, and mansions totalled about 900,000,000 taels, or half a billion dollars. This did not include 56 wonderful pearl necklaces which CH'IA CHING took for himself. As a reward for turning over his treasures HO-SHÊN'S sentence was modified from being hacked to pieces in the market place to permission to hang himself in prison.

Thus ended one of the greatest men in China's long history, rather typically for China. He began as one of Emperor CHIEN LUNG's body guards and rose rapidly to his great estate. His duties included being President of the Boards of Revenue, Appointments, and Punishments. His eldest son married one of Chien Lung's many daughters.

His snuff bottles were, naturally, gifts from many provincial governors and other nobles. Official records indicate they were put up for public sale, with other lesser material, and it is quite possible some of them may be in this collection.

Emperor CHIA CHING was in office from 1796 to 1820, though he had no real authority until the death of CHIEN LUNG, and execution of HO-SHÊN, in 1799. His rule ended a great period of China's prosperity and encouragement of all forms of art in painting, in porcelain, glass, and lapidary masterpieces, and in literature which began under the Manchus during Emperor KANG HSI's long 60 year reign from 1662 to 1722 and continued through the equally great 60 year reign of his grandson CHIEN LUNG 1735-96; which we have seen really ran until his death 1799.

CHIA CHING rigidly forbade any giving of official presents, and this, with the withdrawal of support from the Royal potteries, lapidaries, and other arts pretty definitely ended nearly all fine craft work. (SEE NOTE 19)

All of our really fine snuff bottles were made in this great era of Chinese art, or earlier, and so are real antiques. Snuff was introduced to China in the middle of the seventeenth century, coming by way of Japan. Tobacco smoking had come in 1585 from the Portugese but was banned by Royal decree.

The earliest recorded date on a snuff bottle is 1644 (see one by the same maker dated 1651 in this collection). Some fine porcelain bottles now included in our collections were made much earlier than this but were not originally meant to hold snuff (a lovely one in this collection is from the Ming Dynasty reign of WAN LI, 1573-1619).

There are snuff bottles in our collections made after CH'IEN LUNG's death in 1799. Porcelain bottles bearing later dates are usually inferior in workmanship, and it may be the dates on them can be accepted. Whether all of our porcelain bottles dated Chien Lung or earlier are authentic is questionable; faking of dates was very common and it takes a life long study to know enough about Chinese porcelain to be sure.

There was a nineteenth century revival of fine lapidary work in China for the export trade that produced by modern equipment the wonderfully thin jade work that adorns our great museums. These craftsmen may have also produced some of the hard stone snuff bottles we treasure as being Ch'ien Lung from their fine workmanship. We can not be sure.

It will be noted that the inventory of the HO-SHÊN collection shows it was a "specialised" collection; it included only hard stone and amber bottles and none of porcelain or glass or any other materials. Some modern collections have only ceramic bottles, masterpieces that duplicate not only all the materials & decorations found in larger pieces but also include many rare types of dainty porcelain and earthenware that are to be found only in these snuff bottles.

Many of our fine bottles show by their unmistakably worn condition and repairs that they have seen long service as the treasured possession of some cultured Chinaman. They carried them in the folds of their sleeves, and upon greeting their friends it was the custom to exchange bottles with each other and, with a profound bow, to partake of the friend's brand of snuff. A host would serve snuff at a banquet on the miniature snuff plates which we also collect.

But the record of the HO-SHÊN collection shows clearly that they were also largely prized as wonderful gifts and collectors items for display in their homes. They afforded the amazingly skilled craftsmen of all sorts an ideal OBJET D'ART on which to display their utmost skill, and for two hundred years they produced beautiful bottles made with almost unbelievable patience. They supply a wonderful study for every phase of Chinese art and craftwork of this period is found refined in them.

The most amazing feat in the making of these bottles, outside of the calligraphy painted on the inside of some, is the grinding out of the interiors in the jade and other stone bottles, harder than steel, particularly those of clear rock crystal. There was a task indeed, particularly to do it smoothly up in the shoulders out of reach of the small neck opening. It is not surprising that many opaque bottles are not fully hollowed out for actual use, and this raises the debatable question of whether such bottles are really old or were made for occidental export. The writer is of the opinion that, since the HO-SHÊN record shows positively that these bottles were actively collected in CHIEN LUNG days, that many of these incompletely hollowed bottles were made then, for collectors display only.

There are collections of Chinese snuff bottles in many American homes as well as in our museums. For a home collection they are colorful, dainty, beautiful in their minute detail and fascinating as one grasps the amazing skill and patience in the making they display. A single fine bottle is a charming thing, any collection is in addition so varied in lovely color, form and material as to delight all who see it. And yet it need not dominate the home, as do many other collections. A small case will show a lot of bottles.

The collection partly shown on the pages that follow is planned to eventually include a bottle made of each material or by each technique used by the Chinese for snuff bottles. The collection grows slowly. There are many sources of supply, dealers in Chinese arts, importers, department stores, antique dealers, Chinatown in our cities, and other collectors. But while many bottles are found, particularly of Pekin glass, porcelain, and agate and other hard stones, some of these are obviously made for tourist trade, or, if old, are not of good design. Chinese lapidaries, while wonderful artisans, were not all artists. There is little possibility of a snuff bottle collection becoming static if one collects slowly, always looking for really fine & interesting bottles. This does not necessarily mean high priced, all snuff bottles are surprisingly inexpensive and one finds some startling bargains to add zest to the quest and gloat over.

The museum collections are great sources of information. The collection shown herein owes much to study of the hundreds of fine bottles in the FULLER COLLECTION in the Seattle Art Museum. The Metropolitan Museum of Art at New York has several large lots, (171 in the ALTMAN

COLLECTION); both these Museums will sell photographs of their snuff bottles.

There is an almost total lack of literature on Chinese snuff bottles. This is, as far as is known, the only book on the subject, and there have been only a few magazine articles. Brief references will be found in many fine books on Chinese jade, and porcelains and it is from these and general books on the history, beliefs, and legends of China this book has been made. Since it is intended to be a collectors guide rather than a scholarly treatise references have been omitted. Many statements made herein are debatable, because authorities do not agree, and the information given here appears to be the most reliable. Many notes on motifs have been simplified. An explanation of Chinese beliefs about the dragon, or phoenix, or duality, for instance, would fill many pages. The reader is encouraged to browse further in the libraries.

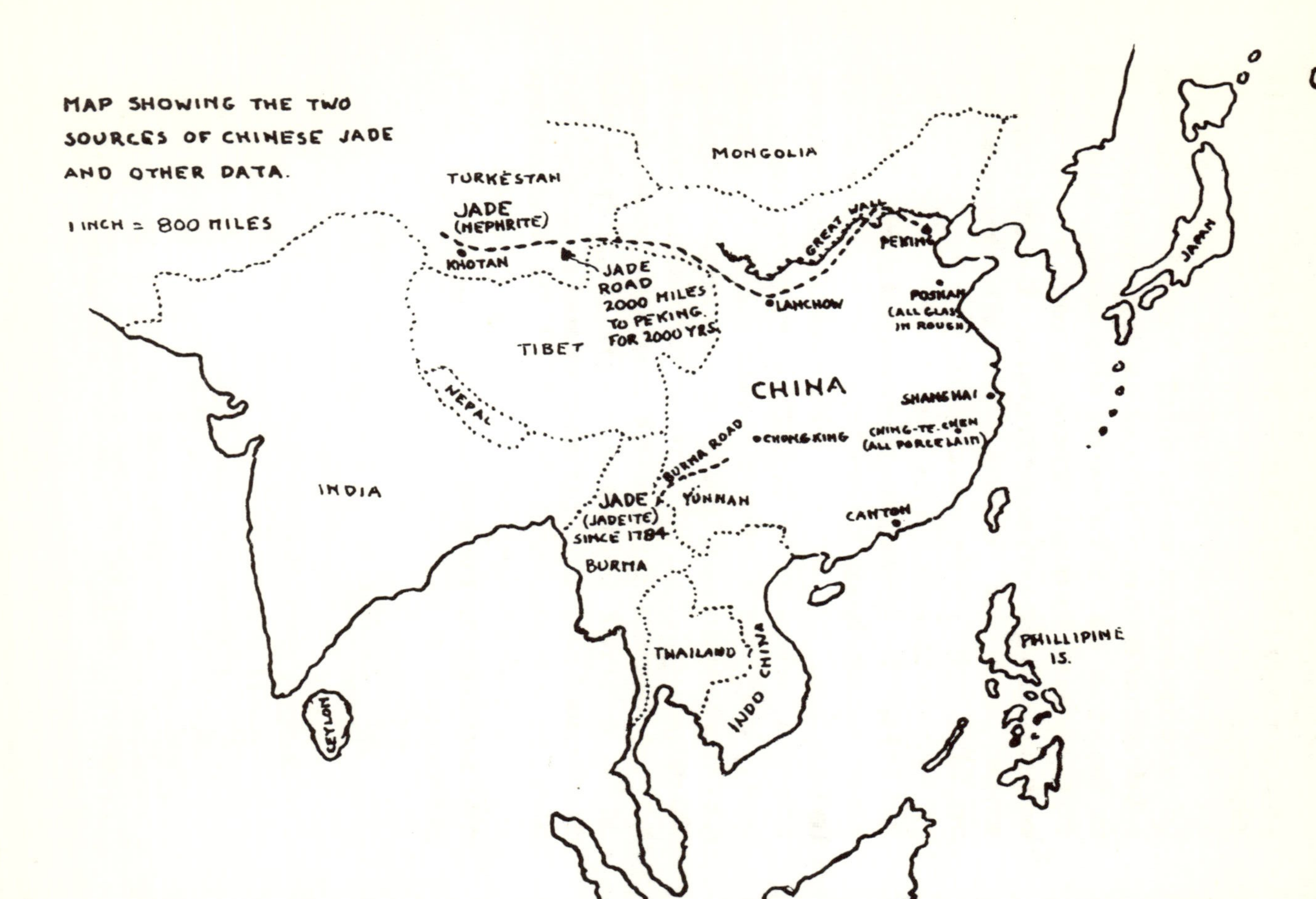
MAP SHOWING THE TWO
SOURCES OF CHINESE JADE
AND OTHER DATA.
1 INCH = 800 MILES
MONGOLIA
TURKESTAN
JADE
(NEPHRITE)
KHOTAN
JADE
ROAD
2000 MILES
TO PEKING
FOR 2000 YRS.
GREAT WALL
PEKING
LANCHOW
POSHAN
(ALL GLASS
IN ROUGH)
TIBET
NEPAL
CHINA
SHANGHAI
CHUNGKING
CHING-TE-CHEN
(ALL PORCELAIN)
BURMA ROAD
INDIA
JADE
(JADEITE)
SINCE 1784
YUNNAN
CANTON
BURMA
THAILAND
INDO CHINA
CEYLON
JAPAN
PHILLIPINE
IS.

CHINESE SNUFF

Is like that of England. finely ground tobaccos mixed with mint, camphor, jasmine, and other aromatic herbs and flowers. It came in a variety of colors, "apple color" and "duck green" being listed as very choice. Some was very high priced because it was claimed to be very old. Large quantities were imported.

The tiny spoon on every snuff bottle stopper was used to ladle snuff on to the left thumb nail, on which it was conveyed to the nose.

Snuff bottles are rarely used in China any more, but medicinal snuff is sold in their drug stores in little bottles like those shown below. A book of 1644-61 says smoking tobacco cures colds and the smoke "goes directly from the mouth to the stomach and passes from within to outside, circulating around the four limbs and the hundred bones of the body", but if the trouble arises from fire inside the body smoking will but inflame it!

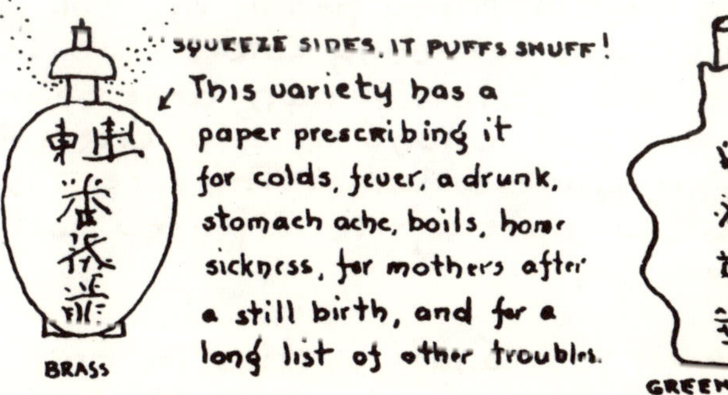

JADE

Nearly twenty-four hundred years ago Confucius said "In Ancient times men found the likeness of all excellent qualities in Jade," and this reverence still continues in China. And strange to say, when the Spanish conquered America, from southern Mexico clear down into South America they found carved jade was there treasured above everything else. And neither in China proper or in these American countries are there any known deposits of jade!

Chinese jade comes either from Eastern Turkestan, by camel train for two thousand miles, or from upper Burma by the famous caravan route. SEE MAP P.8. These are really two entirely different mineral species, nephrite from Turkestan, jadeite from Burma, but so much alike that only an expert can tell them apart and both are called yü or jade by the Chinese. SEE ALSO NOTES 18 AND 14.

Jade is very hard and tough and can be worked only by patient grinding, as described on Page 18. Many people think all jade is green but there are many colors . white, gray, blue, red, yellow, brown, and nearly black, as well as the long series of greens. All have fanciful Chinese names. The rarest is a very beautiful pure white diffused with pale mauve.

Of course jade snuff bottles, in any of the different colors, head any collection in interest.

玉

MADE OF HAN JADE | COLOR GRAY DISCOLORED BROWN

WORKMANSHIP VERY FINE | SIZE, mm 17+60×24 DIA. (4)

PROBABLE REIGN CH'IEN LUNG | DATES 1736-95 (Note 1)

HAS ORIGINAL (2) SPOON-STOPPER OF PINK AGATE, IVORY SPOON

SEE FRONTISPIECE

ACTUAL SIZE (3)

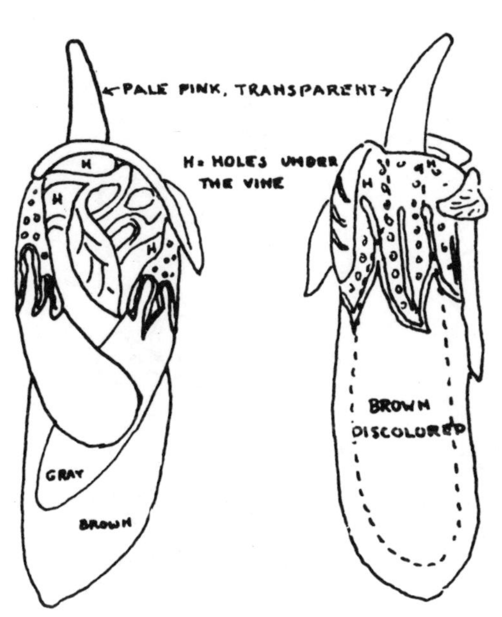

HAN, OR ANCIENT, JADE RECOVERED FROM OLD TOMBS IS MUCH PRIZED. IT IS IDENTIFIED BY ITS DISCOLORATION TO BROWN, RED, AND DARK GRAY THE NAME "HAN" HAS TWO EXPLANATIONS, EITHER FROM A HAN DYNASTY TOMB, 206 B.C. TO 220 A.D.; OR "IN THE MOUTH" AS JADE WAS BURIED IN THE MOUTHS OF DEAD BODIES IN THE BELIEF IT WOULD PREVENT DECAY.

ACQUIRED FROM H. SOOYSMITH, PORTLAND

IN COLLECTION OF HENRY C. HITT

12

MADE OF JADE

COLOR GREEN & BROWN IN SITU

WORKMANSHIP FINE

SIZE, mm 17+50 x 38 x 22 (4)

PROBABLE REIGN CH'IEN LUNG

DATES 1736-95 (Note 1)

HAS ORIGINAL (2) SPOON-STOPPER OF JADE & BROWN, SILVER SPOON

SEE FRONTISPIECE

ACTUAL SIZE (3)

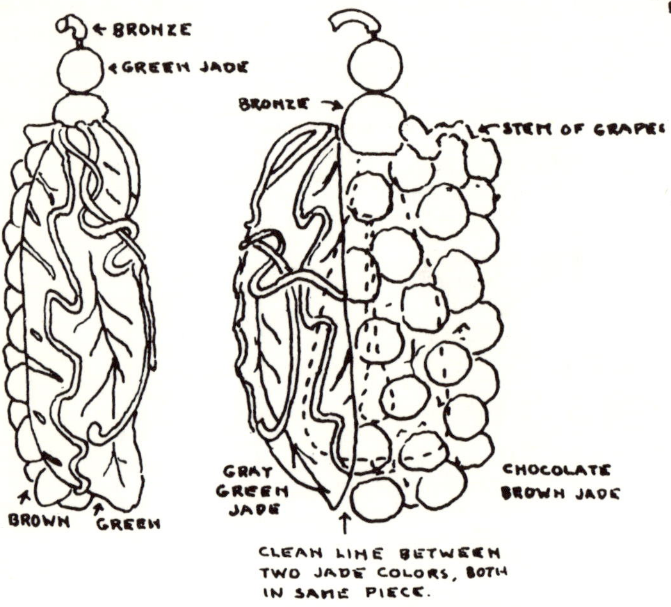

BRONZE

GREEN JADE

BRONZE

STEM OF GRAPES

GRAY GREEN JADE

CHOCOLATE BROWN JADE

BROWN

GREEN

CLEAN LINE BETWEEN TWO JADE COLORS, BOTH IN SAME PIECE.

MOTIFS

A BUNCH OF BROWN GRAPES, WITH A GREEN LEAF, EDGES FOLDED IN, AND COVERED WITH TENDRILS, ALL FROM ONE PIECE OF JADE.

GRAPES WERE INTRODUCED IN CHINA 126 B.C.

ACQUIRED FROM DOLLY MADISON, SEATTLE

IN COLLECTION OF HENRY C. HITT

MADE OF JADE COLOR GRAY

WORKMANSHIP VERY FINE SIZE, mm 5+62×43×25 (4)

PROBABLE REIGN CH'IEN LUNG DATES 1736-95 (Note 1)

HAS ORIGINAL (2) SPOON-STOPPER OF GREEN GEM JADE

CARP ENTWINED IN A LOTUS VINE SEE FRONTISPIECE.

THE CARP IS THE KING OF FISH, CAN CHANGE TO A DRAGON AT WILL, REPRESENTS PROFIT & ABUNDANCE. (6)

LOTUS IS AN EMBLEM OF PURITY, SPOTLESS THOUGH IT ROOTS IN MIRE. (16)

ACTUAL SIZE (3)

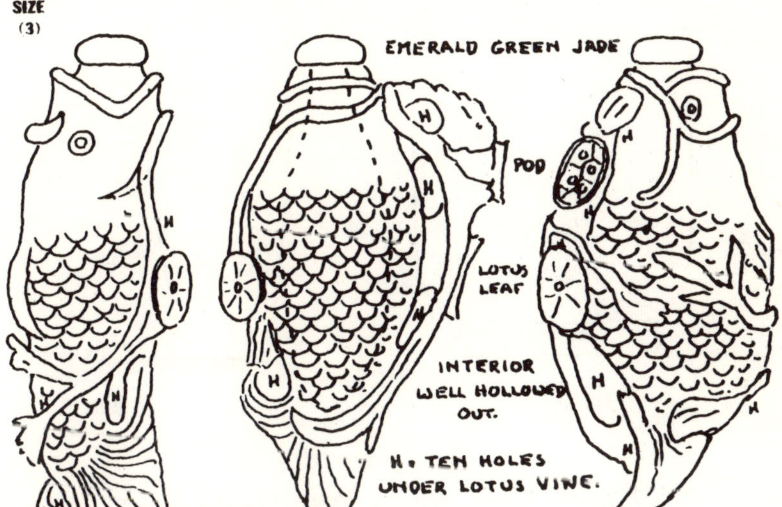

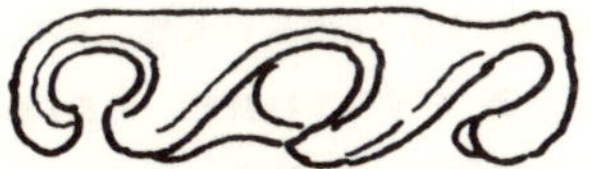

CARPS TAIL HOOKS INTO A TEAK BASE IN WAVE DESIGN, IN ORDER TO STAND UP.

ACQUIRED FROM H SOOYSMITH, PORTLAND.

IN COLLECTION OF HENRY C. HITT

14

MADE OF **JADE**

COLOR GRAYISH MUTTON FAT

WORKMANSHIP INTERIOR ONLY DRILLED

SIZE, mm 7+56×37×15 (4)

PROBABLE REIGN SEE NOTE 5

HAS ORIGINAL (2) SPOON-STOPPER OF BLACK HORN

SEE FRONTISPIECE

ACTUAL SIZE (3)

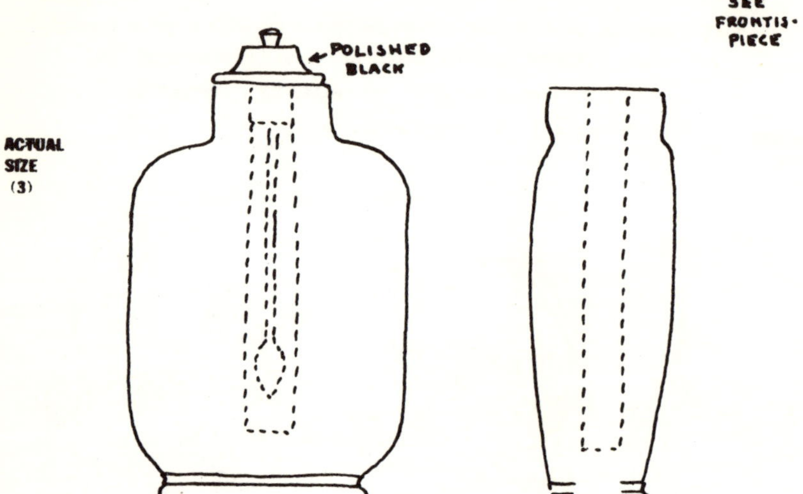

ONE SIDE GRAY WHITE TRANSLUCENT WITH LOOK OF SNOW FLAKES UNDER THE SURFACE. OTHER SIDE IS THE SAME BUT SHOWING ORANGE COLOR WEATHERING. A FEATURE PRIZED BY THE CHINESE AS SHOWING THE BOULDER WAS ANCIENTLY IN A RIVER.

ACQUIRED FROM DOLLY MADISON, SEATTLE.
SET

IN COLLECTION OF HENRY L. HITT

MADE OF **JADE** COLOR SOFT BLUE BROWN STREAK

WORKMANSHIP FAIR, LOW RELIEF SIZE, mm 9+55 x 40 x 31 (4)

PROBABLE REIGN CH'IEN LUNG DATES 1736-95 (Note 1)

HAS ORIGINAL (2) SPOON-STOPPER OF A PEARL, IMITATION CORAL, JADE

← A PEARL

← CORAL GLASS

← YELLOW GREEN

SEE FRONTIS-PIECE.

ACTUAL SIZE (3)

BROWN SHADE IN THIS CORNER

↑
THE MOUSE IS A CREAMY WHITE SPOT, THE ONLY ONE, TYPICAL OF HOW ALL THE CHINESE LAPIDARY DESIGNS FIT MATERIAL.

ACQUIRED FROM CHINATOWN, S.F.

IN COLLECTION OF HENRY C. HITT

MADE OF "CHICKEN-BONE" JADE COLOR CREAM

WORKMANSHIP SUPERB SIZE, mm 53+9×35×18 (4)

PROBABLE REIGN CHIEN LUNG DATES 1735-1796 (Note 1)

HAS ORIGINAL (2) SPOON-STOPPER OF MALACHITE + CORAL

ACTUAL SIZE (3)

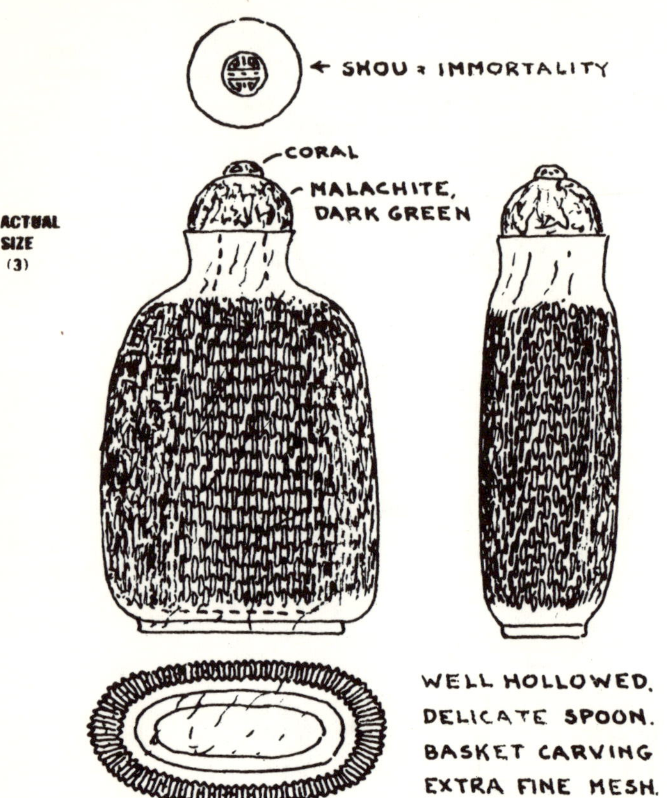

WELL HOLLOWED.
DELICATE SPOON.
BASKET CARVING
EXTRA FINE MESH.

TRUE "CHICKEN BONE" JADE, LOOKS QUITE LIKE CHICKEN BONES, CREAM WITH FAINT BROWN CRACKS. SEE OPPOSITE PAGE →

ACQUIRED FROM H. SOOYSMITH 2-14-46
SFRG

IN COLLECTION OF HENRY C. HITT

MADE OF "CHICKEN BONE" JADE COLOR GRAY

WORKMANSHIP FINE, SMALL HOLLOW SIZE, mm 44+8x27x17 (4)

PROBABLE REIGN DOUBTFUL DATES (Note 1)

HAS ORIGINAL (2) SPOON STOPPER OF GLASS, TOURMALINE, ON BLACK HORN.

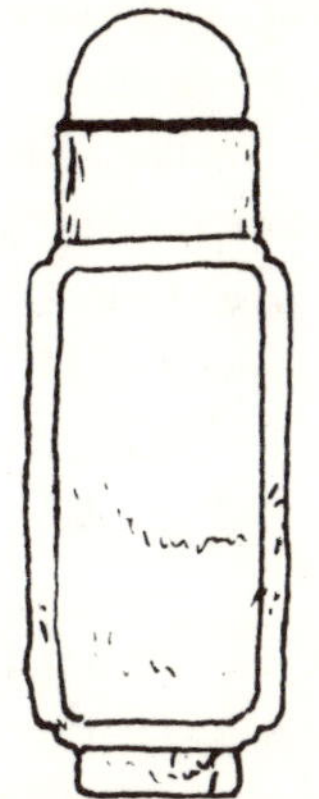

ACTUAL SIZE (3)

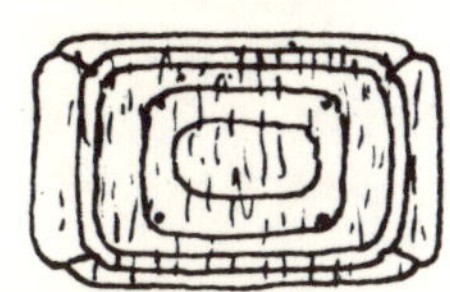

MINUTE CRACKS, FILLED BLACK, GIVE THE LARGE FACES A "HAIR FUR" GRAY APPEARANCE BUT SINCE THE CRACKS ARE ALL PARALLEL THE END FACES ARE CONTRASTINGLY CLEAR WITH FLOCULENT WHITE SPOTS. JADE IS RARELY SO STRATISFIED AS THIS "HAIR FUR" JADE.

CHICKEN BONE JADE

CHI KU PAI

IS JADE THAT HAS BEEN CALCINED AND QUITE CHANGED IN APPEARANCE. IT IS OPAQUE AND FULL OF VERY FINE CRACKS WHICH WHEN FILLED WITH DIRT OR COLOR GIVE A DELICATE SURFACE PATTERN, OFTEN LIKE A NET:-

ACQUIRED FROM H. SOOYSMITH 2-5-46
SURP

IN COLLECTION OF HENRY C. HITT

CHINESE LAPIDARY WORK

All snuff bottles of jade, rock crystal, and other gem and stone materials, and the outside of all glass snuff bottles, have been shaped entirely by patient grinding with sand and water poured over crude foot-driven iron discs and drills; the same way these materials have been wonderfully worked for 3000 years. It is impossible for us to realize such patience. The grinding out of the interiors, around out of reach of the small stopper opening, seems almost impossible.

Jade is brought in big boulders 2000 miles from Turkestan or Burma, and other materials come in odd shaped crystals. The first cutting is done with a wire, patiently pulled back and forth by two Chinese, while a third pours yellow sand on the cut. SEE NOTE 14, MAP P. 8.

A piece when shaped roughly like a snuff bottle is studied by the factory artist, who sketches a design to supply his orders, but conforming cleverly to every flaw or oddity of the piece. If it is jade an effort will be made to show a bit of the discolored outside of the boulder, with the idea it shows age & river origin.

Then the piece goes to the lapidary benches, passing from one to another to suit their set up. These benches are most crude, made of wood and leather with no metal except the metal discs, which carry the sand which does the grinding, and their shaft. The discs are kept turning, or turning back &

forth, by foot treadles. It is all as it has been since before Christ, except that of late years some imported emery sand is used together with the yellow Chinese abrasive. No power and no diamond saws or drills are used, even now.

The final polishing is done with small wheels, less than an inch in diameter, made from the soft wood of a gourd, and takes many more patient hours of work. The gourd wheels are used with wax and gum and last up to ten days.

Amazing indeed is a fine Chinese snuff bottle, or other lapidary piece.

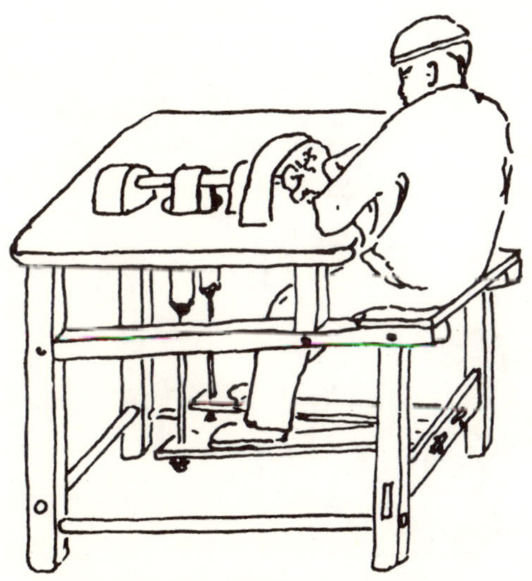

LAPIDARY BENCH AT KHOTAN
(FROM PHOTO IN JADE LORE, GOETTE)

MADE OF TURQUOISE MATRIX

COLOR TURQUOISE & BLACK

WORKMANSHIP FINE, EXCEPT INTERIOR

SIZE, mm 9+41 x 36 x 22 (4)

PROBABLE REIGN SEE NOTE 5

HAS ORIGINAL (2) SPOON-STOPPER OF SAME TURQUOISE

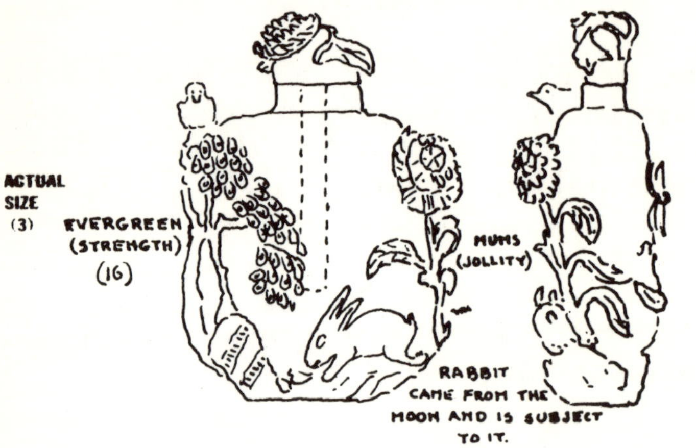

SEE PLATE 1.

SEE NOTE 21

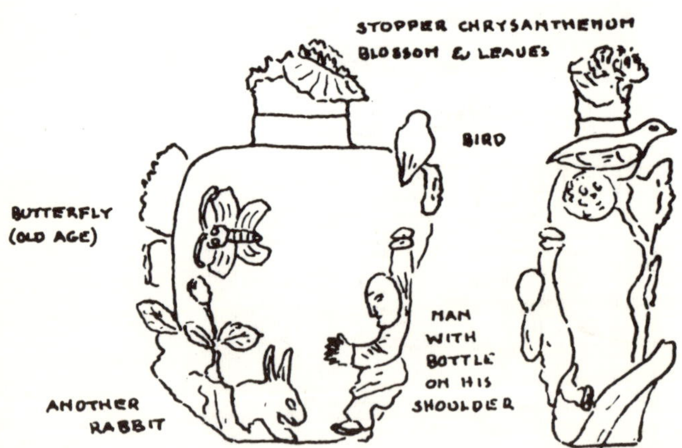

HAS A SPECIAL TEAK BASE.

ACQUIRED FROM MADAME BUTTERFLY, CHINATOWN, S.F.

IN COLLECTION OF HENRY C. HITT

21

MADE OF **AMETHYST** COLOR PURPLE, CLEAR AT BOTTOM

WORKMANSHIP VERY FINE DEEP CARVING SIZE, mm 13+58 x 38 x [illegible] (4)

PROBABLE REIGN CH'IEN LUNG DATES 1736-95 (Note 1)

HAS ORIGINAL (2) SPOON-STOPPER OF SAME AMETHYST AS BOTTLE

SEE PLATE 1.

CRANES IN A LOTUS POND

ACTUAL SIZE (3)

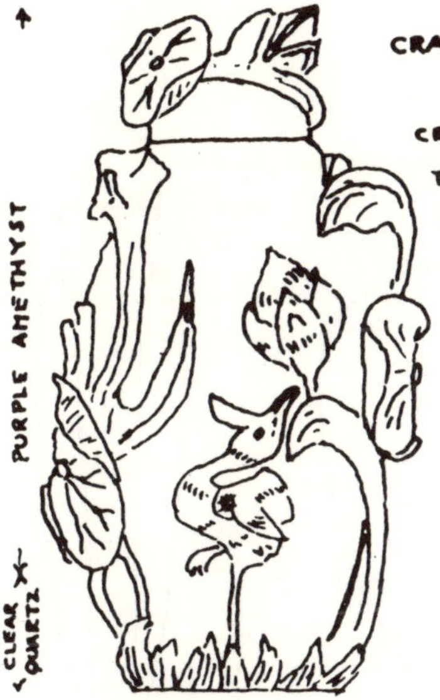

CRANES SIGNIFY LONG LIFE. THEY CARRY TAOIST GODS OFF TO HEAVEN.

(16)

LOTUS = PURITY OF HEART, HAS SPOTLESS PETALS & LEAVES, THO ROOTED IN MUD.

PURPLE AMETHYST

CLEAR QUARTZ

SECTION

ALL THE STEMS AND BIRD LEGS ARE UNDERCUT TO PAPER THIN

HAS A CARVED TEAK STAND

ACQUIRED FROM TATE HENRY, OLYMPIA, WN.
ROGERS

IN COLLECTION OF HENRY C. HITT

22

MADE OF **AGATE** COLOR GRAY, MOTTLED

WORKMANSHIP VERY FINE SIZE, mm 11+54×52×15 (4)

PROBABLE REIGN CH'IEN LUNG DATES 1736-95 (Note 1)

HAS ORIGINAL (2) SPOON-STOPPER OF CLEAR ROSE QUARTZ

SEE PLATE 1

ACTUAL SIZE (3)

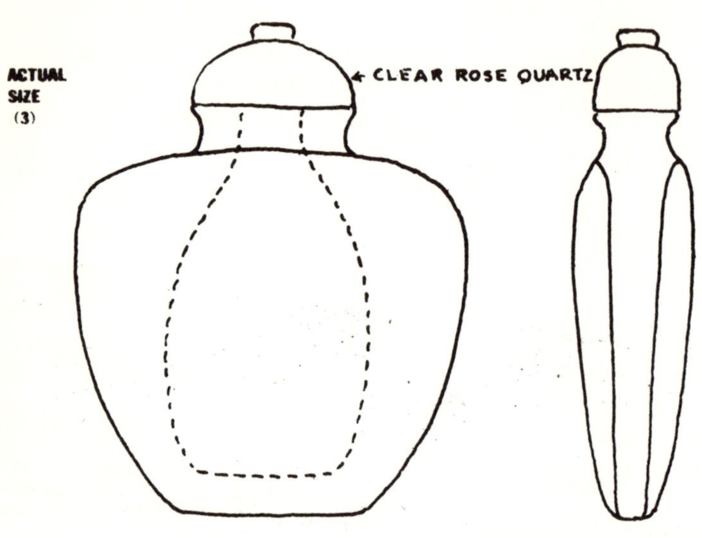

NEEDS NO DECORATION, A VERY BEAUTIFULLY MOTTLED PIECE OF AGATE COVERED WITH INTRICATE GRAY WHORLS, WELL MADE INTO A CHOICE BOTTLE.

ACQUIRED FROM CHINA STORE, PORTLAND, ORE

IN COLLECTION OF HENRY C. HITT

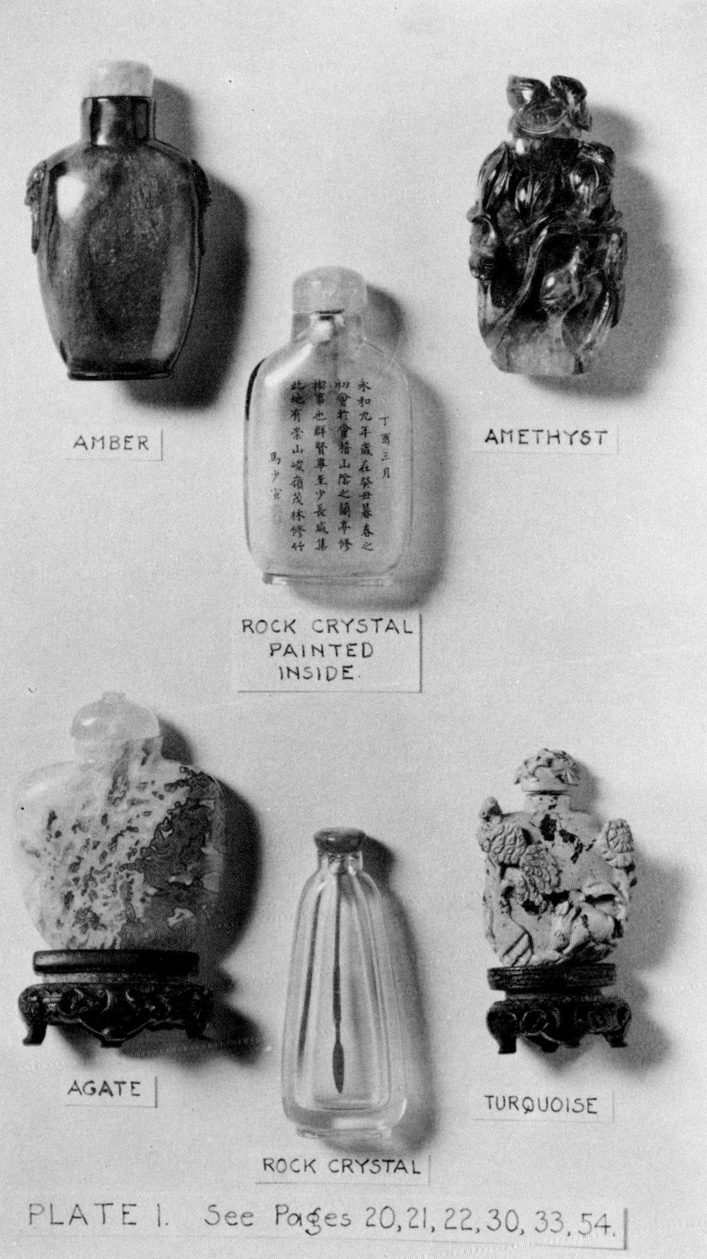

PLATE I. See Pages 20, 21, 22, 30, 33, 54.

24

MADE OF CARNELIAN COLOR ORANGE RED RATHER OPAQUE

WORKMANSHIP NOT WELL CARVED, TWISTED SHAPE SIZE, mm 12+57x40x23 (4)

PROBABLE REIGN LATER THAN CHIEN LUNG.

HAS ORIGINAL (2) SPOON-STOPPER OF CARNELIAN, DARKER THAN BOTTLE.

ACTUAL SIZE (3)

CARNELIAN IS A RED GEM FORM OF AGATE.

ACQUIRED FROM DOLLY MADISON, SEATTLE

IN COLLECTION OF HENRY C. HITT

MADE OF AGATE, MOSS — COLOR GRAY, BROWN MOSS

WORKMANSHIP FAIR, SMALL INTERIOR — SIZE, mm 57×45×27 (4)

PROBABLE REIGN SEE NOTE 5.

HAS ~~ORIGINAL~~? (2) ~~SPOON-STOPPER~~ OF GLASS LIKE GREEN JADE

ACQUIRED FROM WHOLESALER, SEATTLE.

IN COLLECTION OF HENRY C. HITT

MADE OF MARBLE FROM HONAN PROVINCE COLOR GRAY, BANDED

WORKMANSHIP EXCELLENT SIZE, mm 60+10x44x25 (4)

PROBABLE REIGN TAO KUANG DATES 1821-1850 (Note 1)

HAS ORIGINAL (2) SPOON-STOPPER OF HORN AND RED SOAP STONE

ACTUAL SIZE (3)

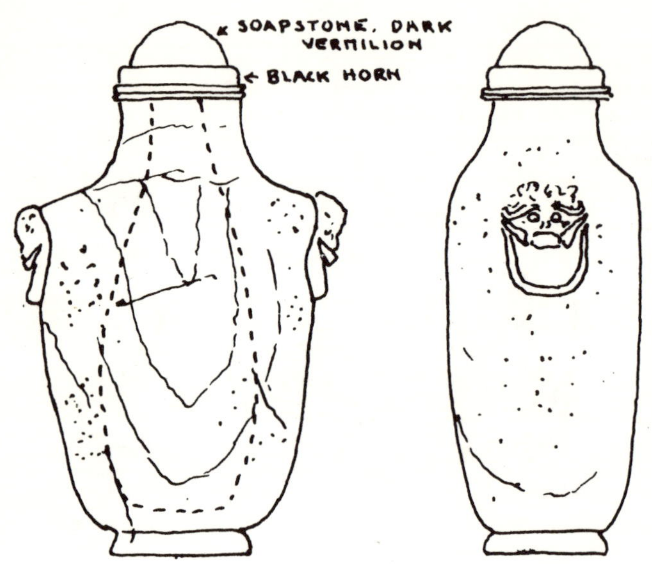

MOTIFS

DOUBLE SIZE DETAIL OF THE UNUSUAL TIGER HEADS. (NOTE 7)

OPAQUE MARBLE IN SHADES OF DARK GRAY BANDED LIKE AGATE AND FLECKED WITH WHITE SPOTS.

ACQUIRED FROM CHRISTMAS PRESENT 1943 FROM H. SOOYSMITH.

IN COLLECTION OF HENRY C. HITT

SOME MOTIFS

YIN AND YANG

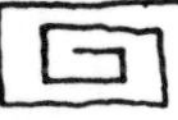

NEGATIVE — POSITIVE

FEMALE — MALE

NIGHT — DAY

JADE IS PERFECT YANG

MTS. THUNDER FIRE EARTH WIND HEAVEN CLOUDS WATER

PA KUA, THE EIGHT TRIGRAMS, WERE SEEN IN 2852 B.C. BY EMPEROR FU HSI ON THE BACK OF A DRAGON HORSE.

FANG SHEN, THE KEY FRET, IS ALSO VERY ANCIENT.

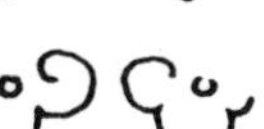

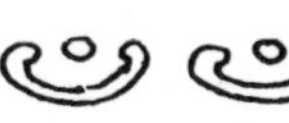

FROM SILKWORM SLEEPING IN COCOON. CLOUDS.

STIFF LEAF — TEMPLE ROOF TILES

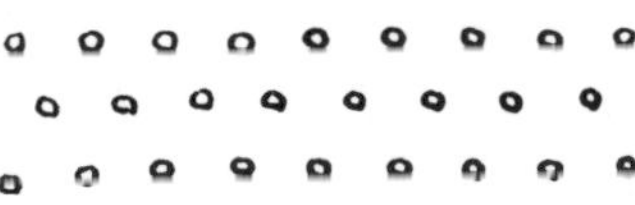

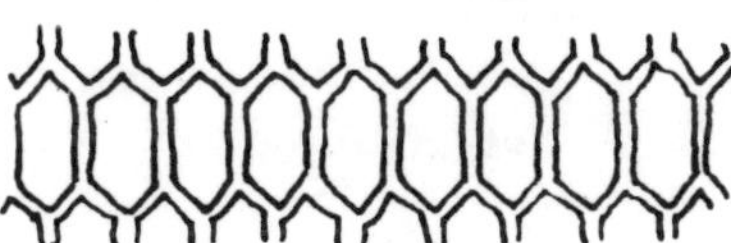

RICE GRAIN PATTERN, IS FOUND ON EARLIEST JADE

MILLET GRAIN. ALSO ANCIENT.

28

MADE OF HAIR CRYSTAL

COLOR DARK SMOKY

WORKMANSHIP VERY FINE

SIZE, mm 10+48x35x20 (4)

PROBABLE REIGN CHIEN LUNG

DATES 1736-95 (Note 1)

HAS ORIGINAL (2) SPOON-STOPPER OF JADE & AMBER

ACTUAL SIZE (3)

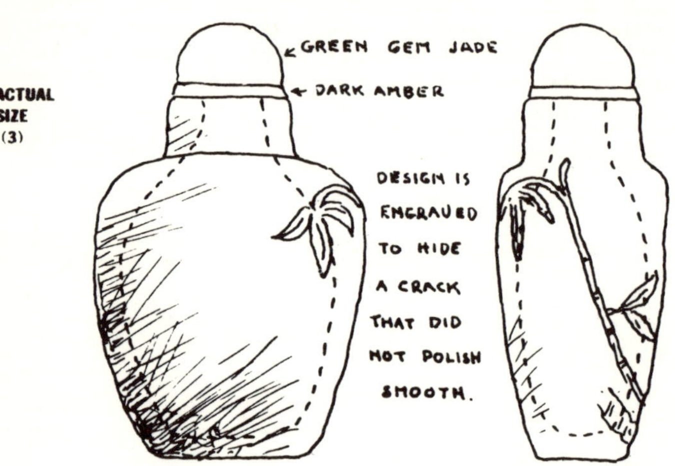

A BEAUTIFULLY MADE BOTTLE OF DARK SMOKY QUARTZ FULL OF HAIR CRYSTALS OF SOME OTHER MINERAL. THERE IS LOTS OF IREDESCENCE WHERE THE HAIRS ARE THICKEST.

ACQUIRED FROM H. SOOYSMITH, PORTLAND.

IN COLLECTION OF HENRY C. HITT

MADE OF ROSE QUARTZ **COLOR** PINK

WORKMANSHIP ONLY FAIR **SIZE, mm** 16+68x60x30 **(4)**

PROBABLE REIGN POSSIBLY MODERN

HAS ORIGINAL (2) SPOON-STOPPER OF SAME ROSE QUARTZ

ACTUAL SIZE (3)

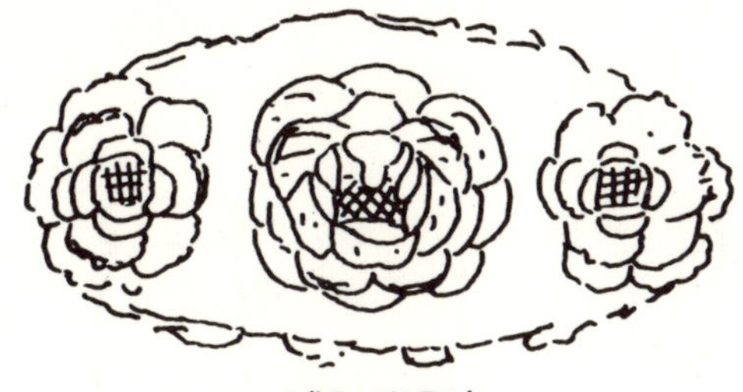

TOP VIEW

OTHER SIDE IS SIMILAR WITH ONE MORE MAGPIE (SIGNIFIES GOOD LUCK)

TREE PEONIES, THE NATIONAL FLOWER, SIGNIFY SPRING, AND ALSO WEALTH.

THE CRANE IS AN EMBLEM OF LONG LIFE.

THUS ALL OF THESE ARE WISHED FOR THE RECIPIENT OF THIS BOTTLE. (16)

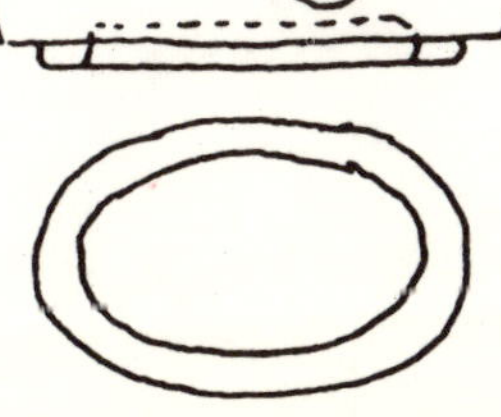

ACQUIRED FROM

IN COLLECTION OF HENRY C. HITT

30

MADE OF ROCK CRYSTAL, SEE NOTE 17 COLOR WATER CLEAR

WORKMANSHIP PERFECT IN SHAPE & FINISH SIZE, mm 4+67×30×16 (4)

PROBABLE REIGN CH'IEN LUNG DATES 1736-95 (Note 1)

HAS ORIGINAL (2) SPOON-STOPPER OF GREEN GEM JADE, RED BONE SPOON

SEE PLATE I.

ACTUAL SIZE (3)

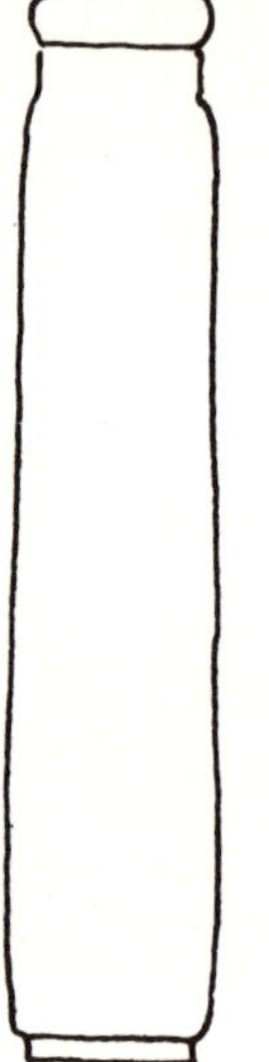

A MARVELOUS BOTTLE, PERFECT IN SYMMETRY, IN FINISH, POLISHED INSIDE AND OUT; FROM A QUARTZ CRYSTAL!

ACQUIRED FROM H. SOOYSMITH, PORTLAND

PAINTINGS on INSIDE of BOTTLES

Painting on the inside of bottles is said to have originated with the great artist Wo TAO-TZU of the Ta'ng Dynasty, 617-906 A.D. It is reported such decoration was done in Canton.

To give a surface to hold paint a mixture of powdered iron oxydul in water was shaken in the bottle for half a day. In painting the artist lies on his back, holding the bottle to the light with his left hand and painting with a crooked brush in his right hand. First he outlines the design in black, then fills in the colors. Many have long inscriptions in fine intricate characters.

Fine painted inside bottles, of glass, rock crystal, and agate, were made in Chien Lung's reign (1736-94) but the wonderful MA SHAO-SÜAN bottles (see next pages) are dated circa 1829-38.

FO-SHOU 佛手 BUDDHA'S HAND CITRON, IS NOT EDIBLE BUT IS FRAGRANT & MUCH PRIZED. OFTEN USED IN DESIGN.

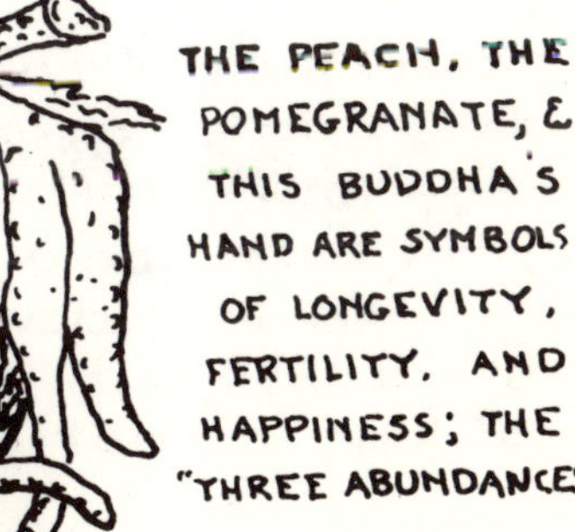

THE PEACH, THE POMEGRANATE, & THIS BUDDHA'S HAND ARE SYMBOLS OF LONGEVITY, FERTILITY, AND HAPPINESS; THE "THREE ABUNDANCES"

The names of few of the artists who worked on Chinese snuff bottles are known; and the few dates found are usually reigns (60 years long for Chien Lung). But in MA SHAO-SÜAN we find a great artist who not only signed but also dated his work.

MA SHAO-SÜAN 馬少宣

He was the master who painted Chinese calligraphy on the inside of snuff bottles circa 1820-1850, often copying scraps of the ancient history of China.

There were fine bottles painted inside in the great CH'IEN LUNG reign of 1735-96 but the bottles of MA SHAO-SÜAN are often mentioned in books as outstanding.

Beautiful calligraphy is the highest art of the Chinese and the studied refinement in every stroke of any of his inscriptions would be marvelous indeed even if it were not also done inside a small necked bottle!

Dr. Berthold Laufer in cataloging the Mrs. Geo. T. Smith collection of snuff bottles in 1913 specially notes the rarity of the three bottles by MA SHAO-SÜAN in that collection. They were No. 403, dated on one side 1822 and on the other autumn 1835 (a puzzle); No. 402 quite like one in this collection and dated only two months later in midsummer 1838; and No. 468 dated 1850, with a genre scene and a typical long inscription.

MADE OF ROCK CRYSTAL (SEE NOTE 17) COLOR SLIGHTLY SMOKY

WORKMANSHIP MARVELOUS, BY MA SHAO-SÜAN SIZE, mm 63+10×40×16 (4)

REIGN TAO-KUANG CYCLICAL DATE: MARCH 1838

(2) SPOON-STOPPER OF GLASS, NOT ORIGINAL

SEE PLATE 1.

ACTUAL SIZE (3)

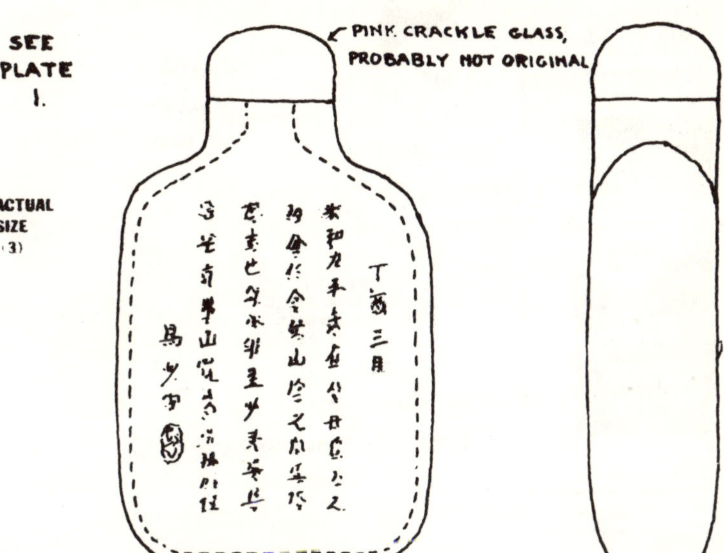

A MA SHAO-SÜAN PAINTED INSIDE BOTTLE DATED, IN CYCLICAL FORM, MARCH 1838.

SEE NEXT PAGE FOR THE DESIGNS ON THE TWO SIDES, DRAWN DOUBLE SIZE AS THEY ARE TOO MINUTE TO COPY ACTUAL SIZE.

SEE OPPOSITE PAGE FOR MA SHAO-SÜAN

ACQUIRED FROM MEI LING, SEATTLE 5-18-43
GLFE

IN COLLECTION OF HENRY C. HITT

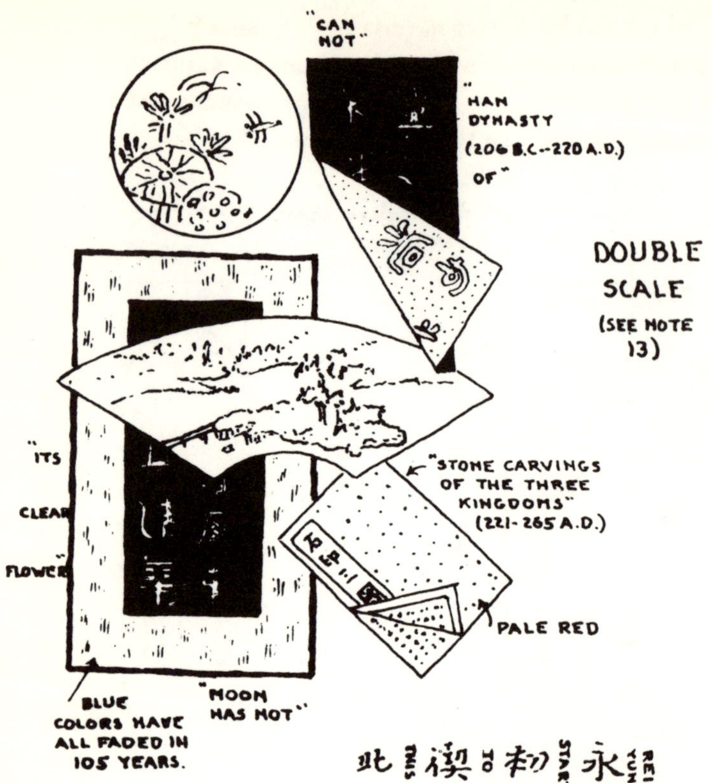

丁酉三月 — CYCLIC DATE TING YU 1838 THIRD MOON

永和九年歲在癸丑暮春之 — REIGN OF YUNG HA 9TH YEAR, CYCLIC YR. FIFTY = A.D. 353, LATE SPRING

初會於會稽山陰之蘭亭修 — START, MET AT CHEKIANG PROVINCE MT, RESTING PLACE

禊事也群賢畢至少長咸集 — TO REPAIR, GROUP OF OFFICIALS CAME, YOUNG OLD GATHERED

此地有崇山峻嶺茂林修竹 — THIS PLACE HAS HIGH MTS, STEEP PEAKS, GREEN TREES, BAMBOO

馬少宣 — MA SHAO-SÜAN

HIS SEAL — VERMILOON, INSCRIPTION BLACK.

MADE OF ROCK CRYSTAL (SEE NOTE 17) COLOR CLEAR

WORKMANSHIP MARVELLOUS, BY MA SHAO-SÜAN SIZE, mm (4)

REIGN TAO KUANG DATES 1829 AUTUMN

HAS ORIGINAL (2) SPOON-STOPPER OF JADE

ACTUAL SIZE (3)

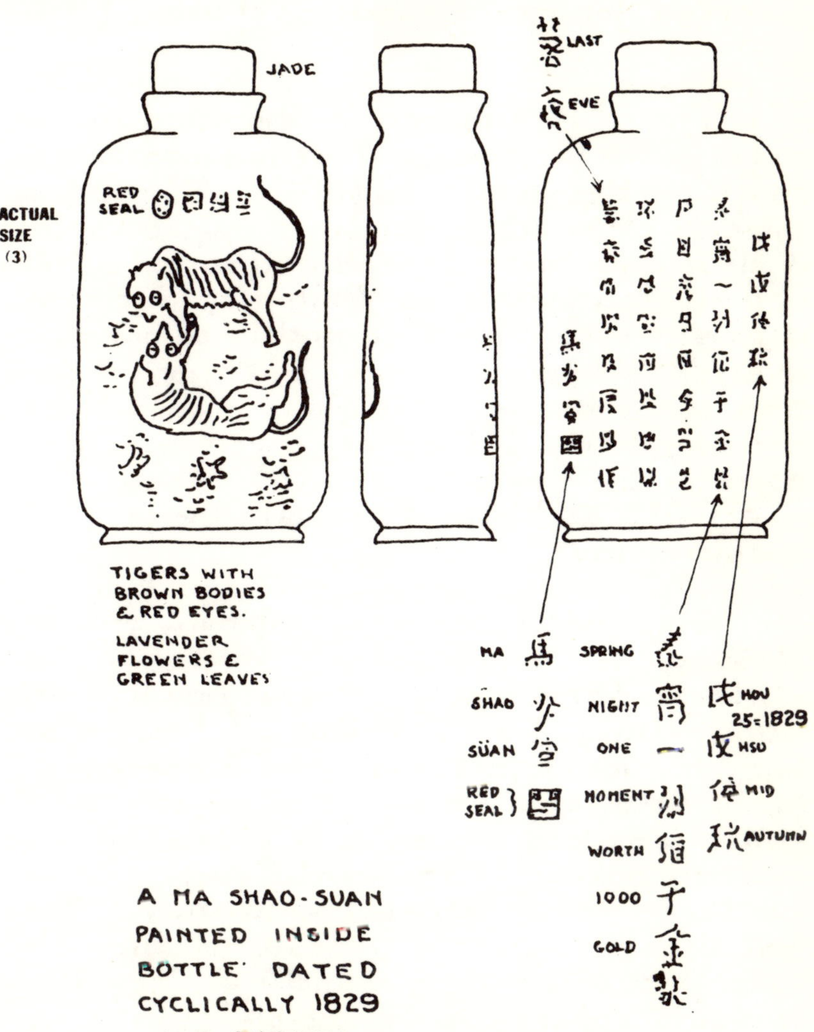

A MA SHAO-SUAN PAINTED INSIDE BOTTLE DATED CYCLICALLY 1829 MID-AUTUMN.

IN COLLECTION OF GRACE F. WICKES, L.A.

GLASS

The manufacture of glass in China dates from A.D. 435 though it had been imported and reworked for many hundreds of years before that

The city of Poshan in Shantung (SEE MAP PAGE 8) is the principal seat of manufacture & snuff bottles in the rough are shipped from there to other cities for finishing; to Canton if clear and to be ground and carved outside and painted inside; to Pekin if of layers of different colors to be carved in cameo style; or elsewhere for the many imitations of gem and stone bottles. All glass snuff bottles are completely ground or carved outside, even for the cheap tourist trade they are never left as blown glass with the original outside glaze.

Glass is treated like any hard gem or stone by the Chinese, a nice material in which to grind lovely designs. And they are wonderfully clever in imitating these other lapidary materials, many an apparently fine jade or gem stone bottle on sale or in collections has proven to be glass. They out-do nature in the lovely colors and patterns they achieve by drawing the hot glass around into designs which are later brought out in grinding. They delight in doing apparently impossible stunts in molding glass

PLUM

MADE OF GLASS, PAINTED INSIDE

COLOR CLEAR GLASS 4 PALE COLORS

WORKMANSHIP EXCELLENT, NOT THE FINEST

SIZE mm 60 × 42 × 33 (4)

PROBABLE REIGN CH'IEN LUNG POSSIBLY

SPOON-STOPPER OF GREEN GLASS

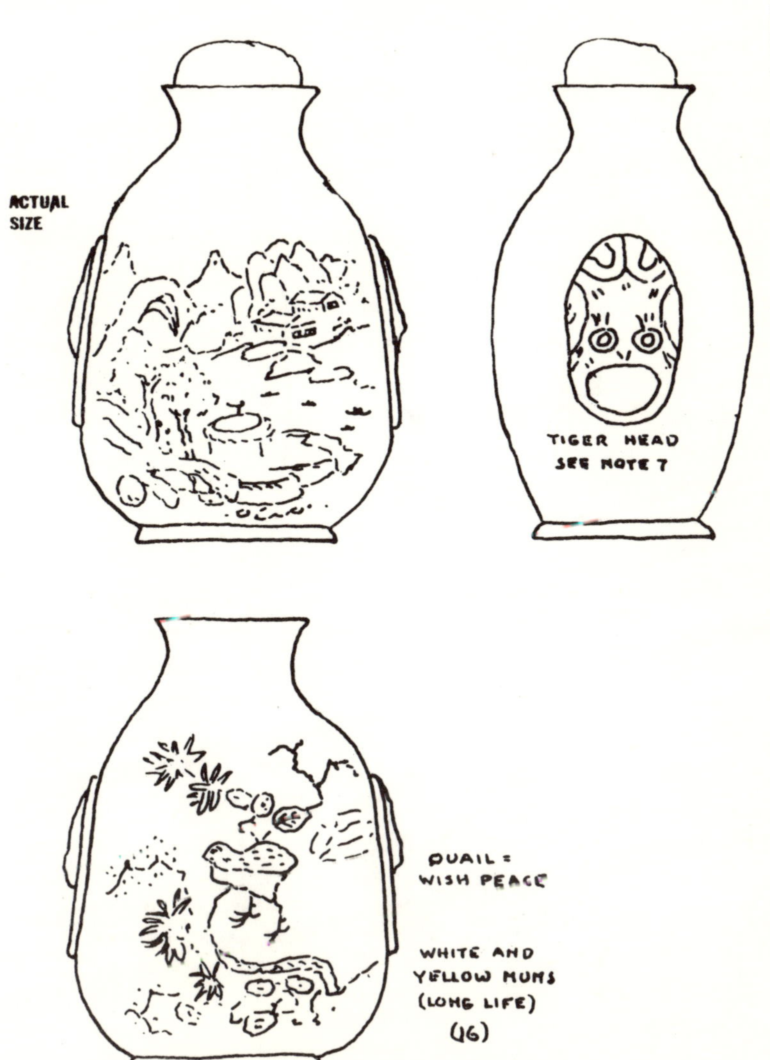

ACQUIRED FROM

IN COLLECTION OF HENRY C. HITT

38

MADE OF GLASS, PAINTED INSIDE **COLOR** CLEAR, BLACK + COLOR

WORKMANSHIP COMMON **SIZE, mm** 10 + 62 × 43 × 25 (4)

PROBABLE REIGN MODERN, TOURIST

HAS ORIGINAL (2) SPOON-STOPPER OF PINK CRACKLE GLASS

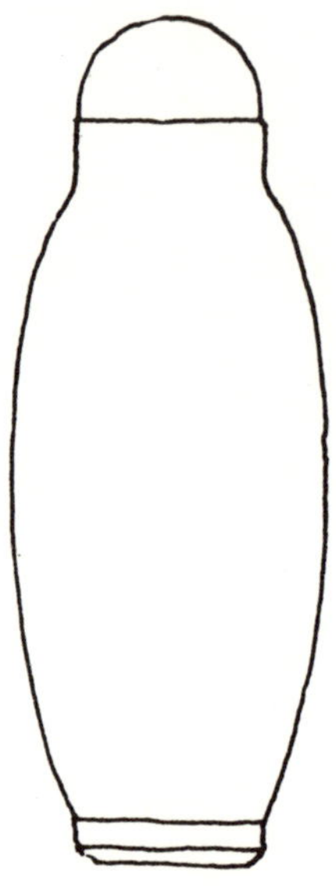

BIRDS DARK BROWN WITH WHITE BREAST

FOLIAGE DARK BROWN, BLUE, GREEN, TOUCHES OF PINK.

IN COLLECTION OF HENRY C. HITT

MADE OF GLASS, PAINTED INSIDE COLOR CLEAR GLASS, 4 COLORS

WORKMANSHIP SCENE DELICATELY PAINTED SIZE, mm 6+64×33×17 (4)

PROBABLE REIGN MODERN, COST 35¢

HAS ORIGINAL (2) SPOON-STOPPER OF GLASS, CRACKLE, BRIGHT PINK

ACTUAL SIZE

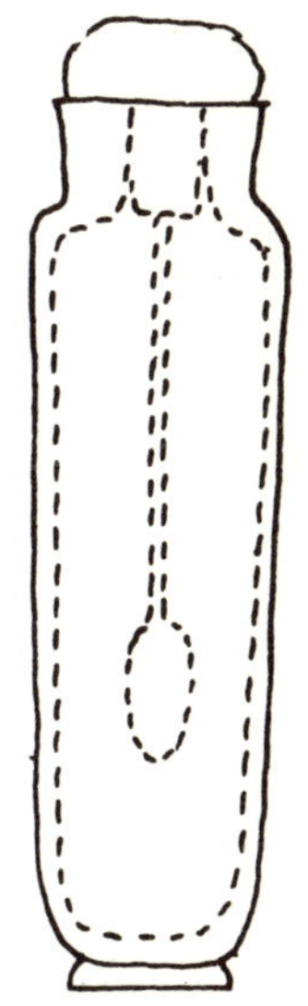

ON OTHER INSIDE

OUTSIDE OF BOTTLE ENTIRELY GROUND TO SHAPE & POLISHED.

MOUNTAIN SCENES DELICATELY PAINTED INSIDE IN 4 COLORS.

AND IT SOLD FOR 35¢ HERE!

ACQUIRED FROM 35¢ AT BON MARCHE, SEATTLE.

IN COLLECTION OF HENRY C. HITT

PLATE 2. See Pages 33, 42, 45, 52, 60, 61.

PEKIN GLASS

This is the usual designation for bottles made in layers of glass of different colors and afterwards cut by lapidaries in cameo style, usually in Pekin, the bottles having been made in Poshan. (See Page 36.)

In the common type (the most plentiful of snuff bottles) an outer colored or black layer of glass is quite thick and is cut to the shapes of the design and itself carved and undercut to leave beautiful designs that appear attached to the contrasting background of the bottle, which is often opaque white, or bubble glass, or a very lovely translucent clear glass clouded with what looks like snow flakes, sometimes called camphor glass. There are many color combinations, designs, shapes, and qualities of this type of Pekin glass, but only two typical bottles will be shown, Pages 42-3.

Sometimes the above type has the design in patches of more than one color. But this is true more often of a much scarcer daintier type where the outer colored layers of glass are very thin and the deep carving to make the design stand out is mostly cut into the bottle glass (usually opaque white) with exquisite carving of the thin colored glass to bring out minute detail. Some of these dainty bottles are signed with a seal and are apparently the work of one artist lapidary, not at all the usual manufacture.

MADE OF PEKIN GLASS COLOR BLUE ON SNOWFLAKE

WORKMANSHIP VERY FINE, DEEPLY UNDERCUT SIZE, mm 8+59x50x23 (4)

PROBABLE REIGN CH'IEN LUNG DATES 1736-95 (Note 1)

HAS ORIGINAL (2) SPOON-STOPPER OF ROSE QUARTZ, FINE IVORY SPOON

SEE PLATE 2.

ACTUAL SIZE

THE POET LI T'AI PO, A.D. 701-62 GETTING INSPIRATION FROM A PINE TREE, HIS SERVANT WITH HIS WRITING BOX READY BEHIND HIM.

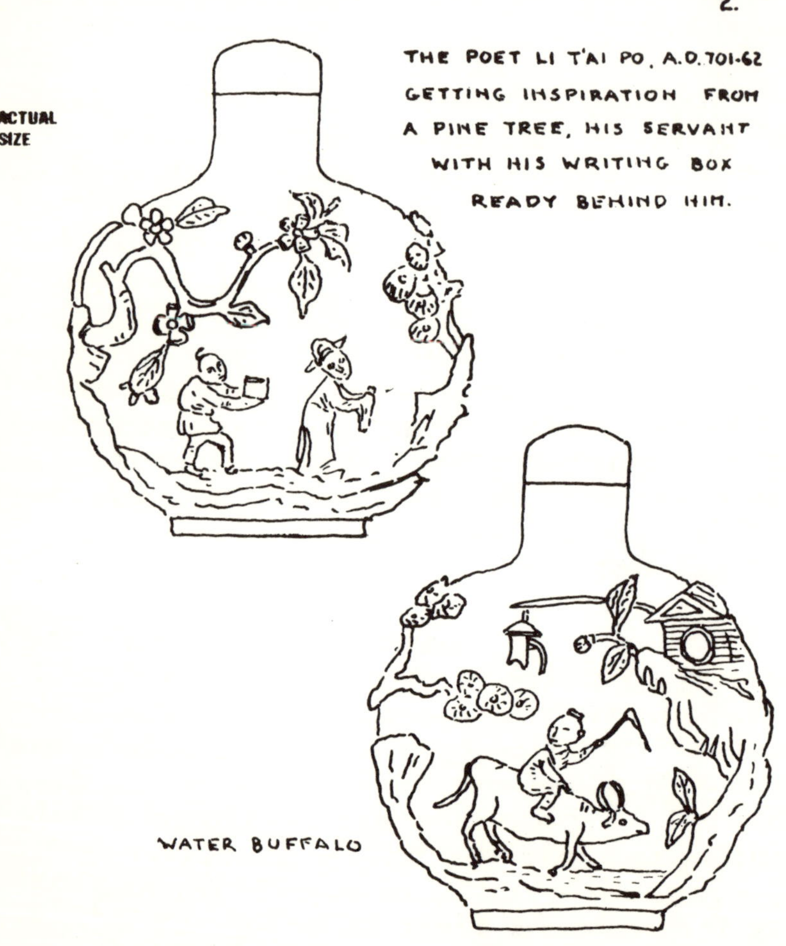

WATER BUFFALO

ACQUIRED FROM MEI LING, 5TH AVE., SEATTLE

IN COLLECTION OF HENRY C. HITT

MADE OF PEKIN GLASS COLOR BLUE ON SNOW FLAKE

WORKMANSHIP EXCELLENT SIZE, mm 8+64x52x30 (4)

PROBABLE REIGN CH'IEN LUNG DATES 1736-95 (Note 1)

HAS ORIGINAL (2) SPOON-STOPPER OF GREEN JADE

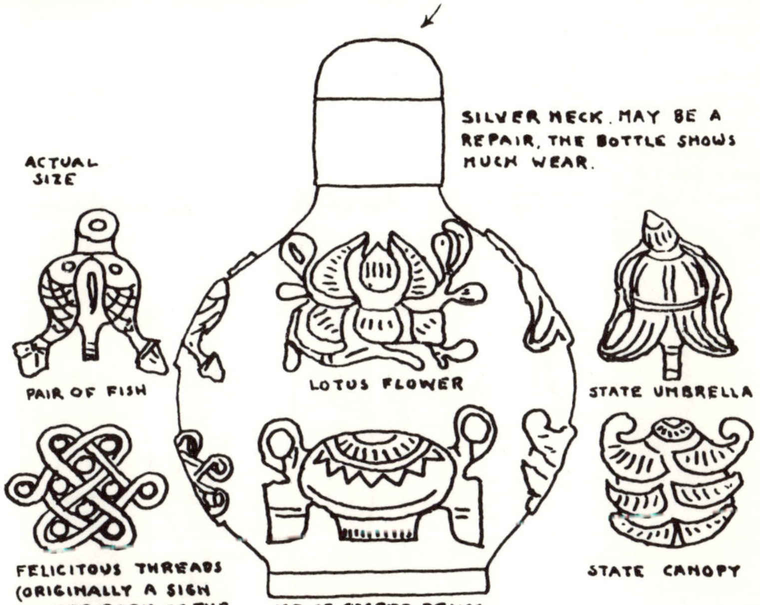

SILVER NECK. MAY BE A REPAIR, THE BOTTLE SHOWS MUCH WEAR.
ACTUAL SIZE
PAIR OF FISH
LOTUS FLOWER
STATE UMBRELLA
FELICITOUS THREADS (ORIGINALLY A SIGN ON THE BODY OF THE HINDU GOD VISHNU)
JAR OF SACRED RELICS
STATE CANOPY

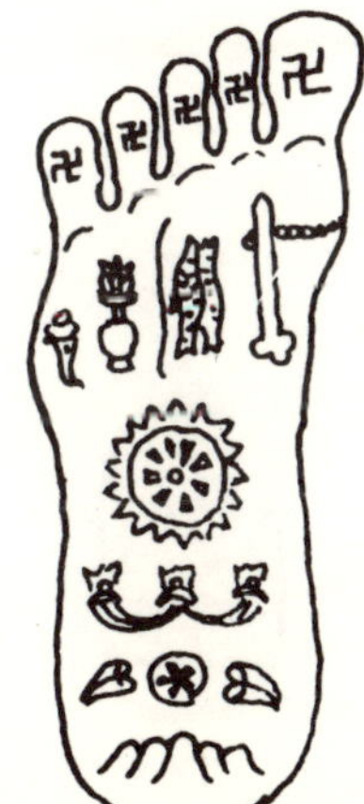

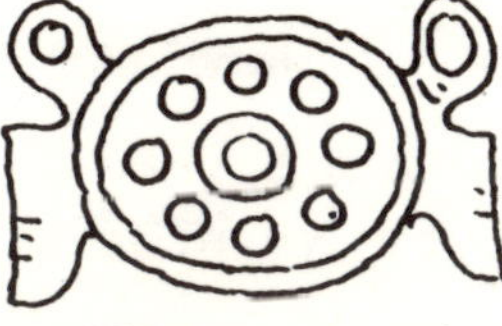

WHEEL OF THE LAW
CONCH SHELL TRUMPET FOR RELIGIOUS FESTIVALS

EIGHT OF THE 108 SYMBOLS SUPPOSED TO HAVE IMPRINTED ON THE SOLE OF BUDDHA'S FOOT. OPPOSITE IS ONE FOOTPRINT WITH PART OF THE 108. NOTE THE 卍 A SIGN OF GREAT ANTIQUITY IN CHINA AND INDIA.

卐 SWASTIKA 卍 SUAVASTIKA

卍 NINE TIMES 卐 ONCE, ON BUDDHA'S FOOTPRINT.

ACQUIRED FROM H. SOOYSMITH

IN COLLECTION OF HENRY C. HITT

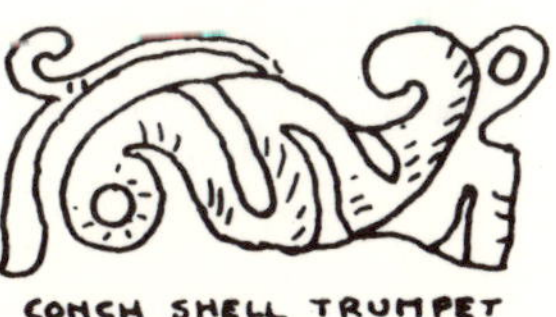

MADE OF PEKIN GLASS, SEAL TYPE COLOR BLUE ON WHITE

WORKMANSHIP SUPERB, DAINTY SIZE, mm 7+64 × 31× 14 (4)

PROBABLE REIGN CH'IEN LUNG DATES 1735-96 (Note 1)

HAS ORIGINAL (2) SPOON-STOPPER OF CARNELIAN.

ACTUAL SIZE (3)

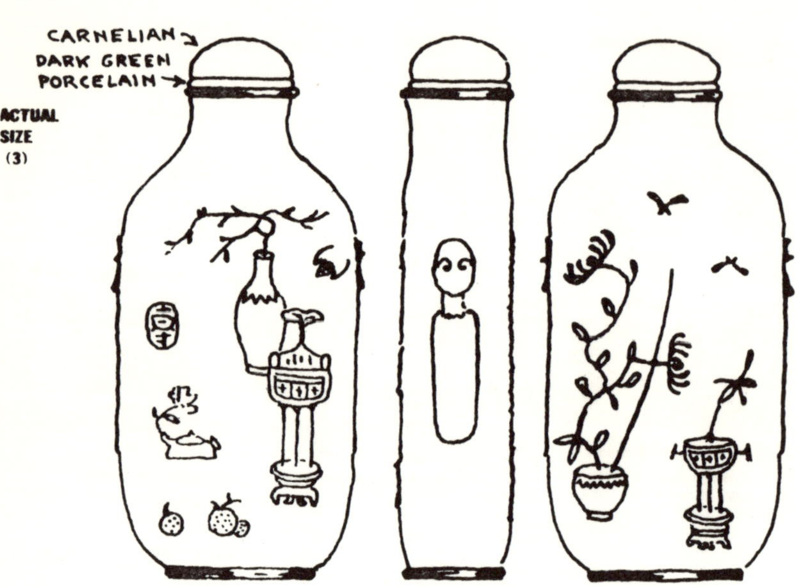

BOTTLE OPAQUE WHITE GLASS
THIN OVERLAY BLUE GLASS

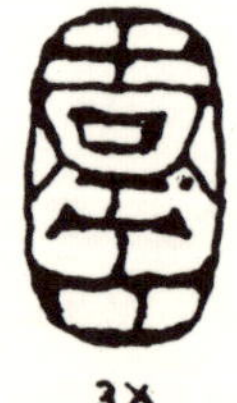

3X

ACQUIRED FROM MRS. GERTRUDE STUART 10-1-44
BEG

IN COLLECTION OF HENRY C. HITT

MADE OF PEKIN GLASS, SEAL TYPE COLOR POLYCHROME ON WHITE

WORKMANSHIP SUPERB, DAINTY SIZE, mm 8+59×34×26 (4)

PROBABLE REIGN CH'IEN LUNG DATES 1735-96 (Note 1)

HAS ORIGINAL (2) SPOON-STOPPER OF EMERALD GREEN JADE

ACTUAL SIZE (3)

COLORS, THIN GLASS OVERLAY

B = OLIVE BROWN

G = TURQUOISE GREEN

P = PINK

O = CREAMY ORANGE

ON OPAQUE WHITE GLASS.

SEE PLATE 2.

3X

ACQUIRED FROM MRS. GERTRUDE STUART 10-1-44
OFU

IN COLLECTION OF HENRY C. HITT

MADE OF CORAL IMITATION COLOR CORAL RED

WORKMANSHIP FAIR SIZE, mm 62+7×40×28 (4)

PROBABLE REIGN LATER THAN CH'IEN LUNG DATES (Note 1)

HAS ORIGINAL (2) SPOON-STOPPER OF CORAL

ACTUAL SIZE (3)

MOTIFS OBVERSE

CHRYSANTHEMUMS. SYMBOLS OF JOLLITY

THIS BOTTLE IS AN EXTREMELY GOOD GLASS IMITATION OF CORAL, EVEN TO CHARACTERISTIC SMALL HOLES. THE COLOR IS PERFECT, BUT IT IS TOO HARD, HCl ACID DOES NOT EAT IT, IT HAS GLASS FLOW LINES.

ACQUIRED FROM CHINA STORE, 3RD AVE., SEATTLE. XSFE

IN COLLECTION OF HENRY C. HITT

MADE OF GOLDSTONE COLOR BROWN, GOLD SPARKLES

WORKMANSHIP VERY FINE SIZE, mm 10+46×43×19 (4)

PROBABLE REIGN SEE NOTE BELOW DATES (Note 1)

HAS ORIGINAL (2) SPOON-STOPPER OF METAL, WITH GEMS

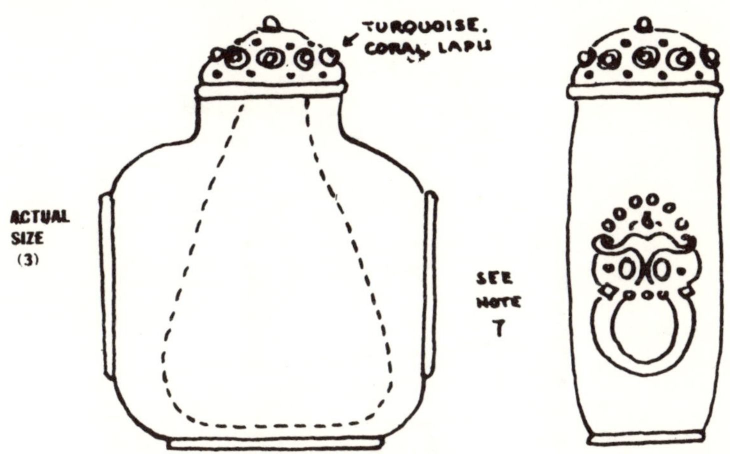

ACTUAL SIZE (3)

SEE NOTE 7

GOLDSTONE, CHOCOLATE BROWN FULL OF GOLD SPARKLES, IS A GLASS FROM CZECHO-SLOVAKIA INTRODUCED TO THE OCCIDENT AT THE CHICAGO WORD'S FAIR IN 1893 AND SINCE AVAILABLE FOR LAPIDARY USE. THE CHINESE VARIETY APPEARS IDENTICAL AND THEY MAY IMPORT IT. ABOVE BOTTLE IS APPARENTY DRILLED OUT, NOT MOLDED INSIDE

OPAQUE GLASS BOTTLES

ABOVE BOTTLE IS SOMEWHAT TYPICAL OF A LONG SERIES OF LUSTROUS OPAQUE GLASS BOTTLES ENTIRELY WITHOUT ORNAMENT, OR WITH TIGER HEADS ONLY AS ABOVE, THAT ARE BEAUTIFUL BECAUSE THEY ARE MADE OF FLAWLESS GLASS IN LOVELY COLORS AND ARE SUPERBLY SHAPED AND POLISHED. THE COLORS, USUALLY MONOCHROME, IMITATE VERY CLOSELY MANY SHADES OF JADE AND CELADON PORCELAIN AND ARE DEEP AND RADIANT. SO MANY OF THESE BOTTLES SHOW NO SIGNS OF WEAR IT APPEARS THEY MUST BE COMPARATIVELY MODERN.

ACQUIRED FROM CHINA STORE, VANCOUVER, B.C.

IN COLLECTION OF HENRY C. HITT

48

MADE OF GLASS, OPAQUE

COLOR MAROON

WORKMANSHIP MOTTLED GLASS, AMAZING

SIZE, mm 9+62×42 DIA.

PROBABLE REIGN UNCERTAIN

HAS ORIGINAL (2) SPOON-STOPPER OF HORN & CORAL GLASS, SILVER SPOON

ACTUAL SIZE

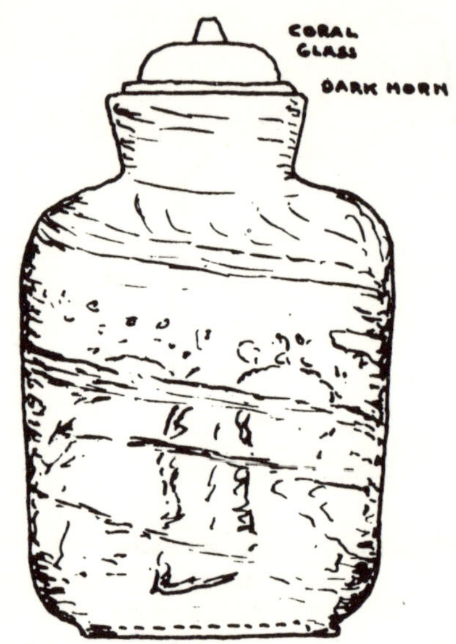

AN INTERESTING BOTTLE IN THE WAY THE OPAQUE GLASS, MAROON WITH STREAKS OF LIGHT AND VERY DARK, HAS BEEN DRAWN AROUND INTO A VERY FINE PATTERN THAT WAS ONLY VISIBLE AFTER THE BOTTLE WAS GROUND TO SHAPE

ACQUIRED FROM PRESENT FROM H. SOOYSMITH

IN COLLECTION OF HENRY C. HITT

MADE OF GLASS COLOR CLEAR, RED GOBS

WORKMANSHIP VERY FINE & CURIOUS SIZE, mm 10+58x46x30 (4)

PROBABLE REIGN CH'IEN LUNG DATES (Note 1)

HAS ORIGINAL (2) SPOON-STOPPER OF MALACHITE & CORAL

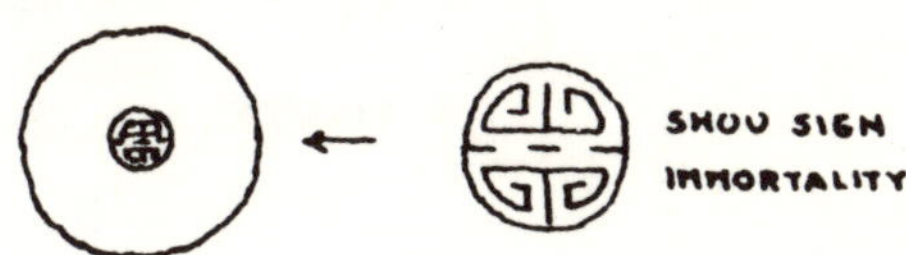

ACTUAL SIZE

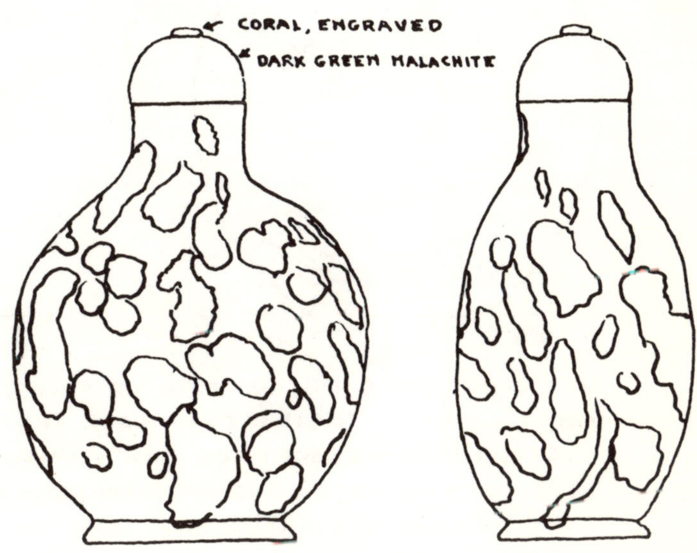

A CURIOUS TRICK OF GLASS BLOWING. CLEAR GLASS EXCEPT FOR GOBS AS SHOWN OF OPAQUE DARK RED. INSIDE OF BOTTLE IS BUMPY BUT OUTSIDE HAS BEEN GROUND SMOOTH THROUGH ALL THE GOBS.

ACQUIRED FROM H. SOOYSMITH

50

MADE OF GLASS

COLOR GRAY, BLACK MARKINGS

WORKMANSHIP FINE & VERY PUZZLING

SIZE, mm 7+57x 53 x 25 (4)

PROBABLE REIGN CH'IEN LUNG

DATES 1735-96 (Note 1)

HAS ORIGINAL (2) SPOON-STOPPER OF JADE IN SILVER

ACTUAL SIZE (3)

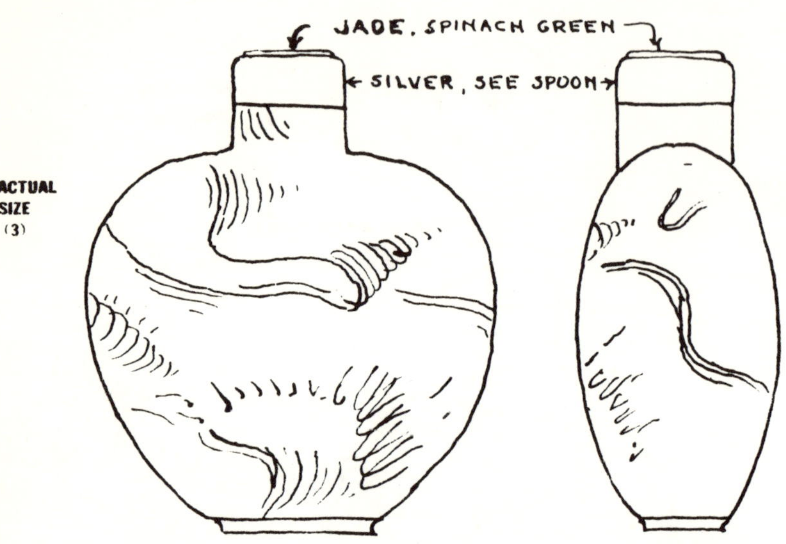

VERY PUZZLING DECORATION OF FINE BLACK PAINT LINES IN SERIES THAT LOOP FROM JUST UNDER THE SURFACE DOWN UNDER IN MOST INTRICATE INTERESTING PATTERNS. THE GLASS IS TRANSLUCENT GRAY.

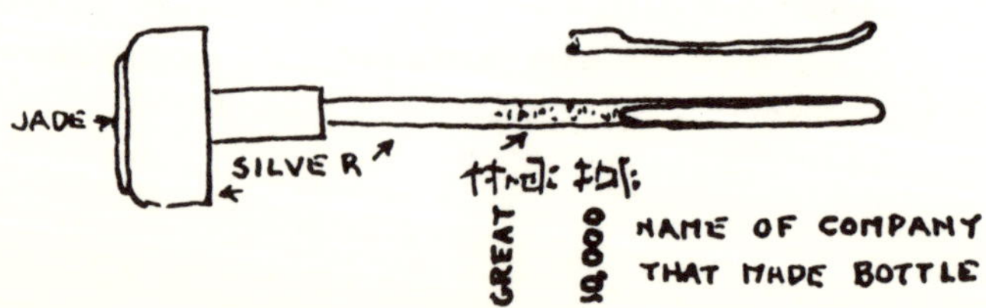

ACQUIRED FROM H. SOOYSMITH 3-9-44
ASAR

IN COLLECTION OF HENRY C. HITT

MADE OF GLASS, WITH GOLD LEAF
COLOR DARK, WITH GOLD FLECKS

WORKMANSHIP GOOD, VERY UNUSUAL
SIZE, mm 9+65×45×20 (4)

PROBABLE REIGN CH'IEN LUNG
DATES 1736-95 (Note 1)

HAS ORIGINAL (2) SPOON-STOPPER OF JADE AND BONE

ACTUAL SIZE

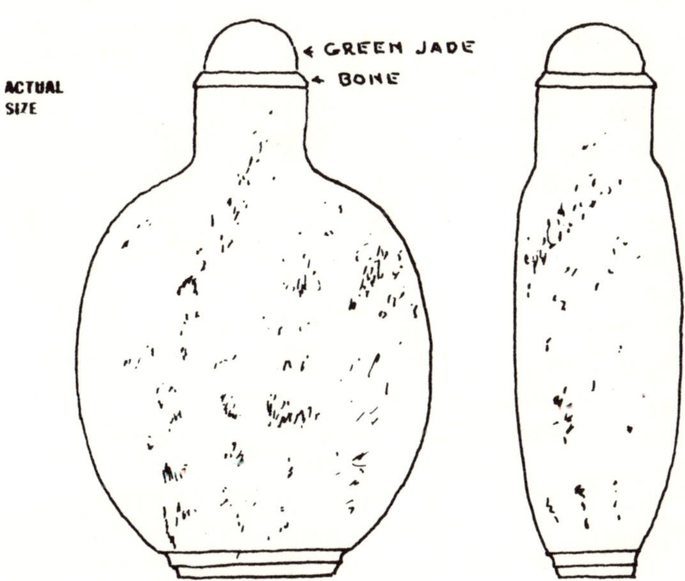

THIN DARK GLASS WITH FLECKS OF GOLD LEAF THROUGH IT. TRANSLUCENT, A DARK TEA COLOR, SOME OF THE GOLD LEAF IS SO THIN IT, TOO, IS TRANSLUCENT. THE OUTSIDE IS GROUND & POLISHED ALL OVER, AS ALWAYS ON A CHINESE SNUFF BOTTLE.

ACQUIRED FROM H. SOOYSMITH

MADE OF KU-YÜEH HSÜAN GLASS COLOR CÂFE AU LAIT

WORKMANSHIP SUPERB SIZE, mm 57+11×57×20 (4)

PROBABLE REIGN CH'IEN LUNG DATES 1735-1796 (Note 1)

HAS ORIGINAL (2) SPOON-STOPPER OF TURQUOISE, & YELLOW HORN.

KU-YÜEH HSÜAN OR "ANCIENT MOON PAVILION" was the studio name of the great Director Hu of the Imperial glass works established in Pekin in 1680.

His glass was so lovely Emperor Chien Lung was said to have ordered Tang Ying, Director of Imperial potteries to match it, and so originated the loveliest and rarest of porcelain also called Ku-Yüeh Hsüan

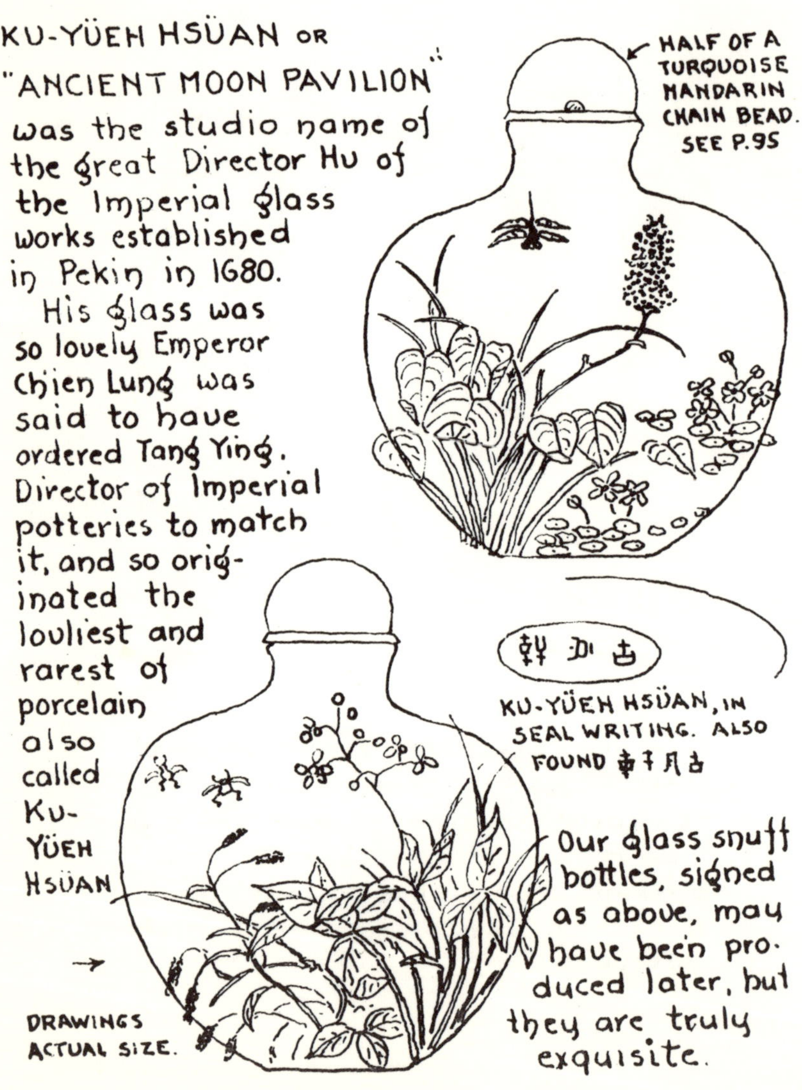

Our glass snuff bottles, signed as above, may have been produced later, but they are truly exquisite.

DRAWINGS ACTUAL SIZE.

ACQUIRED FROM NBED H. SOOYSMITH 7-18-46

MADE OF HORNBILL BEAK — COLOR YELLOW & CRIMSON

WORKMANSHIP FINE, DEEP RELIEF — SIZE, mm 60+10x 50x 15 (4)

PROBABLE REIGN CH'IEN LUNG — DATES 1735-1796 (Note 1)

HAS ORIGINAL (2) SPOON-STOPPER OF OPAQUE GLASS, CORAL RED.

ACTUAL SIZE (3)

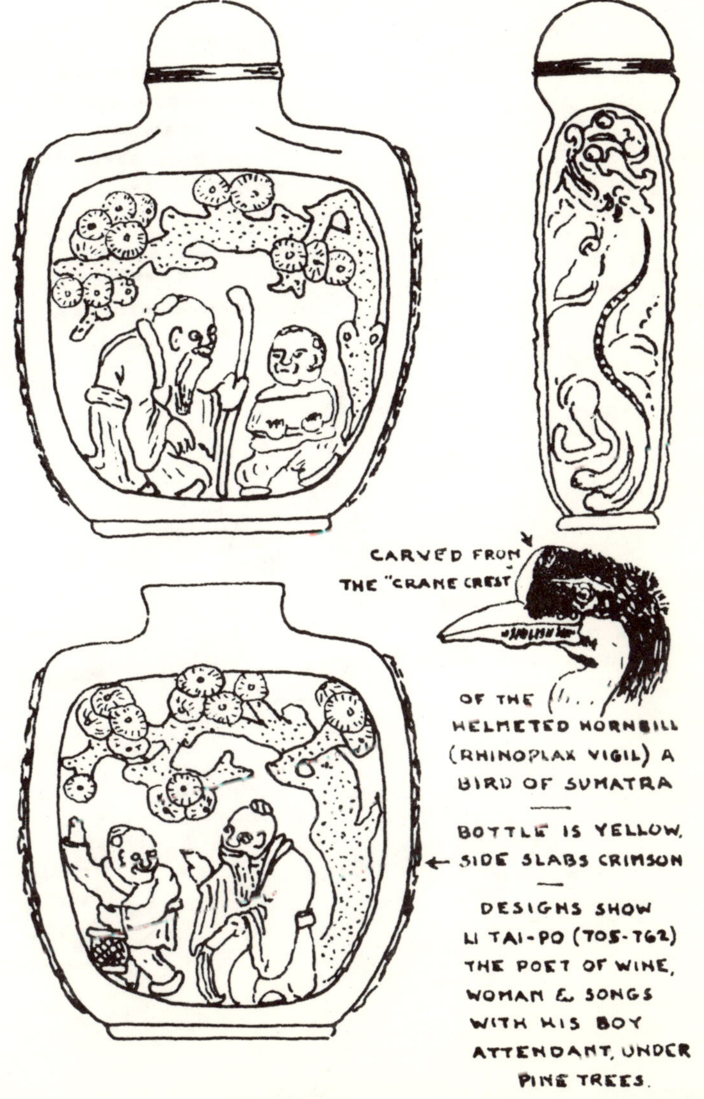

IN FULLER COLLECTION, SEATTLE ART MUSEUM

52

MADE OF ENAMEL ON GLASS, WHITE TRANSLUCENT COLOR 6 COLORS

WORKMANSHIP FINE SIZE, mm 6+38×33×18 (4)

PROBABLE REIGN CH'IEN LUNG DATES 1735-96 (Note 1)

HAS ORIGINAL (2) SPOON-STOPPER OF CORAL

COLORS

OPAQUE BROWN BLACK
" GREEN BLACK
" VERMILION
" BLUE GREEN
BROWN WASH
BLUE "

ON TRANSLUCENT WHITE GLASS.

CORAL STOPPER.

ACTUAL SIZE (3)

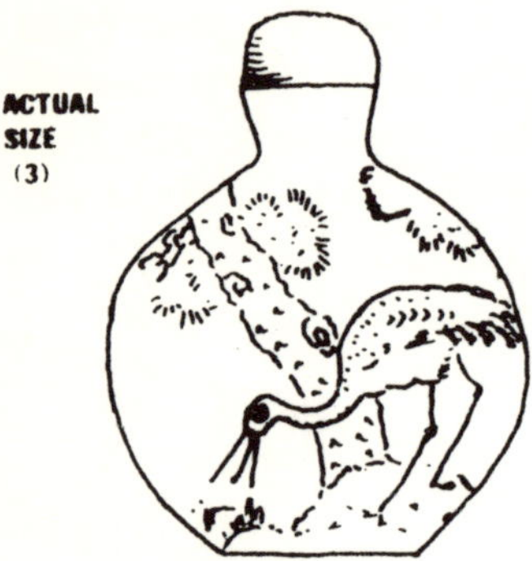

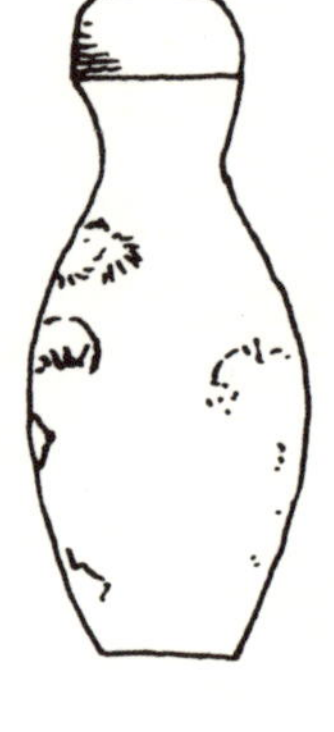

NO ATTEMPT CAN BE MADE TO COPY THE MINUTE BRUSH WORK.

SEE PLATE 2

ACQUIRED FROM MRS. GERTRUDE STUART, 10-1-48
NER

IN COLLECTION OF HENRY C. HITT

AMBER

Amber is a fossil gum of prehistoric pine trees. It is brittle and takes a high polish, but can be scratched with a knife. It feels warm to the touch, and attracts paper when rubbed. The principal world supply is from East Prussia, but all Chinese amber came from Burma. In color Burmese amber runs from cream yellow to dark red, & from clear to cloudy. A rare fiery and red variety is called "gold amber" by Chinese. All amber snuff bottles appear to have been made by lapidary methods, not carved by edged tools. SEE MAP. P.8.

IVORY

Elephants were native in China 2000 years B.C., and captive until recently. An empress of the Chou Dynasty, 1112-247 B.C., had five kinds of chariots, decorated with jade, gold, ivory, leather, and wood. African ivory is called best, but mammoth, walrus, and narwhal ivory is also used. Walrus ivory dyed green with verdigris to simulate jade is often found used in the stoppers of snuff bottles.

54

MADE OF AMBER | COLOR ORANGE BROWN

WORKMANSHIP EXTREMELY FINE | SIZE, mm 9+67x44x22. (4)

PROBABLE REIGN CHIEN LUNG | DATES 1736-95 (Note 1)

HAS ORIGINAL (2) SPOON STOPPER OF GREEN GEM JADE, FINE AMBER SPOON

ACTUAL SIZE (3)

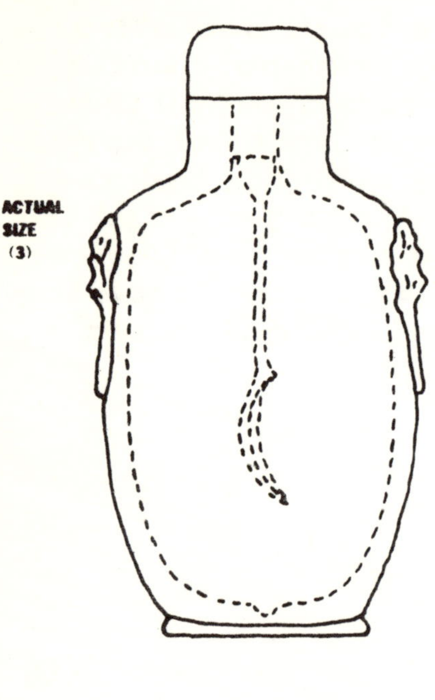

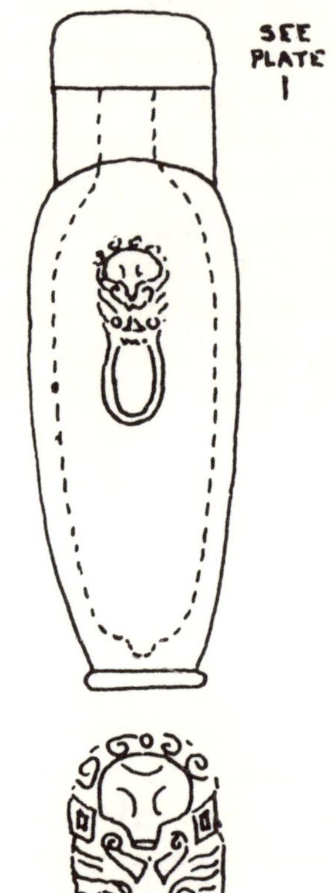

SEE PLATE 1

A BEAUTIFULLY MADE BOTTLE, EXQUISITE IN EVERY DETAIL, VERY THOROUGHLY HOLLOWED OUT, LOVELY SPOON, SEE PAGE 91.

DOUBLE SIZE DETAIL OF TIGERS HEAD ON BOTH SIDES (NOTE 7)

ACQUIRED FROM H. SOOYSMITH

MADE OF IVORY COLOR IVORY, COLORED

WORKMANSHIP FINELY CARVED & COLORED SIZE, mm 99 OVER ALL x 25 x 17 (4)

REIGN DATED CH'IEN LUNG DATES 1736-95 (Note 1)

HAS ORIGINAL (2) SPOON-STOPPER OF HEAD IS STOPPER, LONG IVORY SPOON

HSI-WANG MU

QUEEN MOTHER OF THE WESTERN PARADISE. HER GARDEN GREW PEACHES THAT CONFERRED IMMORTALITY, RIPENING IN 3000 YEARS.

CHIEN LUNG DATE

MAY BE A JAPANESE FORGERY.

ACQUIRED FROM OLD CURIOSITY SHOP, SEATTLE

SAW A DUPLICATE AT ROSENBACHS, PHILADELPHIA

IN COLLECTION OF HENRY C. HITT

MADE OF IVORY, ENGRAVED **COLOR** IVORY

WORKMANSHIP FINE, ENGRAVING MICROSCOPIC **SIZE, mm** +51x41x13 **(4)**

PROBABLE REIGN IVORY TOO LIGHT TO BE OLD. **DATES** **(Note 1)**

HAS ORIGINAL (2) SPOON-STOPPER OF IVORY

ACTUAL SIZE (3)

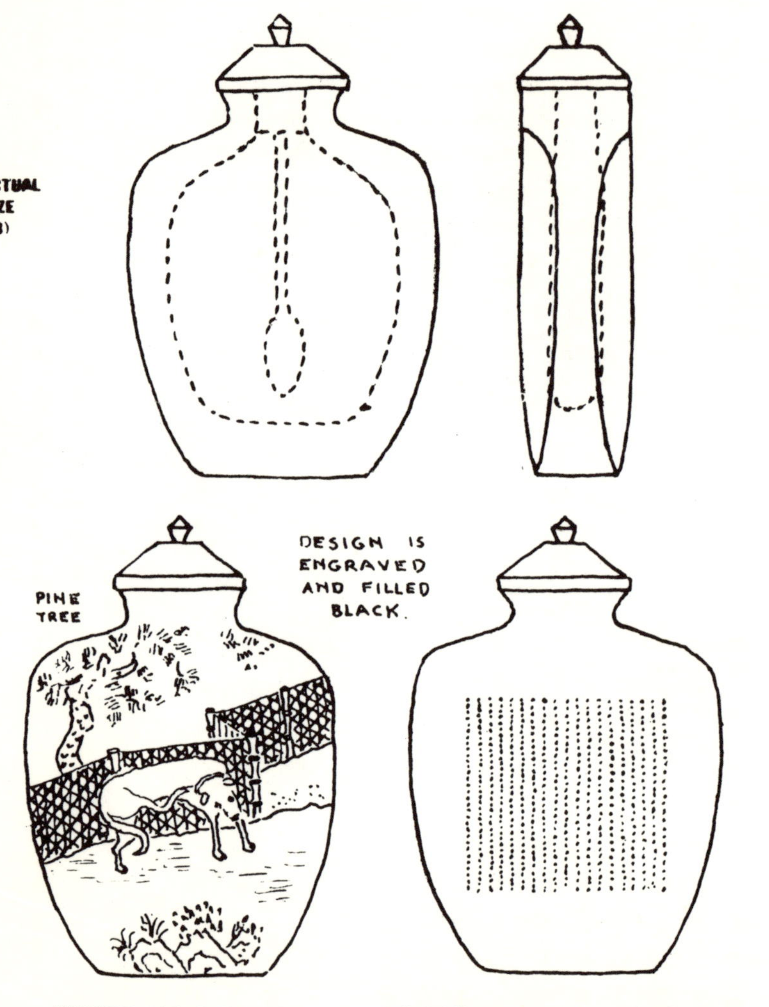

HOUNDS WERE RAISED IN CHINA BEFORE 200 B.C.

IN ONE SQUARE INCH 688 VERY COMPLICATED CHINESE WRITING CHARACTERS! SEE NEXT PAGE.

ACQUIRED FROM CHINESE STORE, PORTLAND, ORE.

IN COLLECTION OF HENRY C. HITT

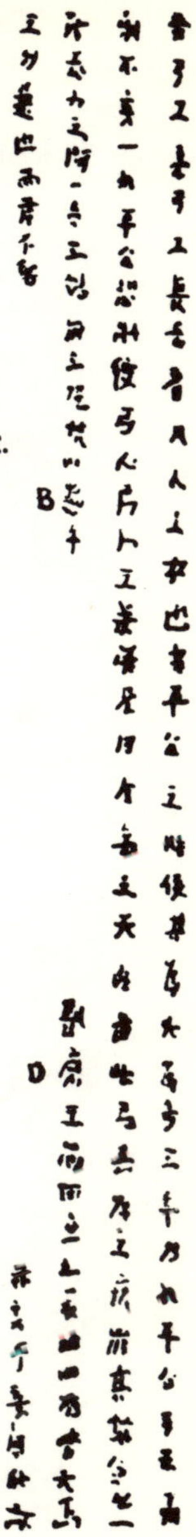

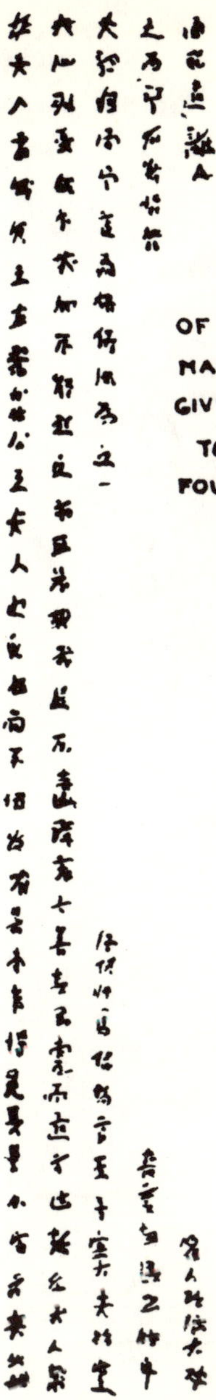

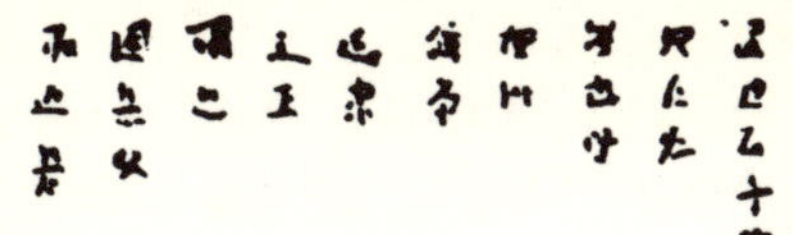

THE BORDER SHOWS CRUDE DRAWINGS OF 285 OF THE 688 CHARACTERS, MAGNIFIED 6X, SIMPLIFIED BUT GIVING THE GENERAL APPEARANCE. TO SHOW THE MICROSCOPIC DETAIL FOUR CHARACTERS ARE DRAWN 20X

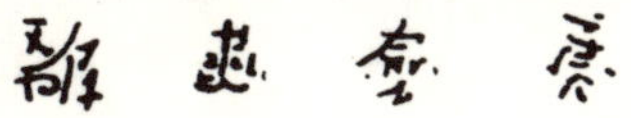

A B C D

58

MADE OF IVORY COLOR DARK WITH AGE

WORKMANSHIP FINE, FIGURES IN FULL RELIEF SIZE, mm 13+53×31×24 (4)

PROBABLE REIGN CH'IEN LUNG DATES 1736-95 (Note 1)

HAS ORIGINAL (2) SPOON-STOPPER OF IVORY

ACTUAL SIZE

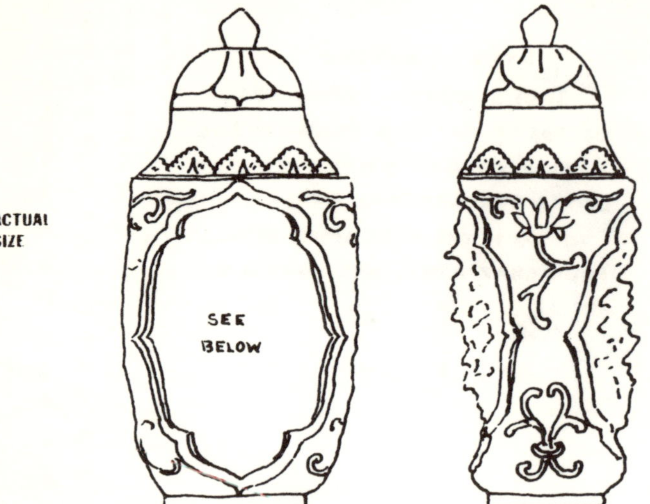

TWO TAOIST PRIESTS SEARCHING FOR LING CHIH, SACRED FUNGUS, SYMBOL OF IMMORTALITY

CARVINGS IN HIGH RELIEF

ACQUIRED FROM DOLLY MADISON, SEATTLE

IN COLLECTION OF HENRY C. HITT

CERAMIC BOTTLES

Chinese pottery dates back to 3000 B.C., and porcelain to the Tang Dynasty, 618-906 A.D..

All ceramic snuff bottles were probably made at CHING-TÊ-CHÊN, 300 miles southwest of Shanghai, either in the Imperial or in private potteries. (SEE MAP P.8) It has been the great center of porcelain manufacture since 1369 A.D.. Ceramic snuff bottles may be very old, like the Ming bottle on the next page, if originally made for uses other than snuff.

Most porcelain bottles are dated, but early dates may not be authentic, as "the heathen Chinee is peculiar." Deciding the dates of porcelain by glaze, coloring, design, or workmanship is a fascinating study, with many beautiful books and museum collections to help but still full of puzzles.

Every ceramic bottle is enchanting in its beauty, the interest of its design, and the problem of its age; and a large collection of ceramic snuff bottles alone would be wonderful, as it would probably show every type of Chinese porcelain for the last three centuries in their most delicate perfection. Indeed, some exquisite types of porcelain are not found except in snuff bottles.

MADE OF PORCELAIN, THIN
COLOR WHITE, FAINT BLUE GRAY DESIGN
WORKMANSHIP IMPERIAL POTTERS
SIZE, mm 10+54 x 36 DIA. (4)
REIGN WAN LI, MING DYNASTY
DATES 1573-1619 (Note 1)
HAS ORIGINAL (2) SPOON-STOPPER OF CORAL & YELLOW GLASS

SEE PLATE 2

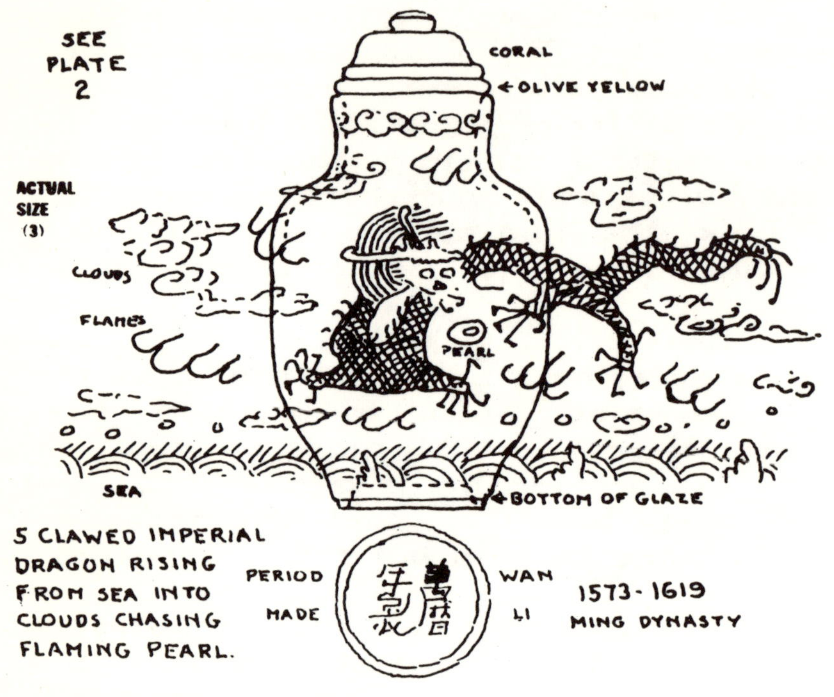

5 CLAWED IMPERIAL DRAGON RISING FROM SEA INTO CLOUDS CHASING FLAMING PEARL.

PERIOD MADE 萬曆年製 WAN LI

1573-1619 MING DYNASTY

AN IMPERIAL MING VASE, LATER CONVERTED INTO A SNUFF BOTTLE.

THIN, TRANSLUCENT, PURE WHITE, WITH DESIGN INCISED IN THE BASE PORCELAIN, COLORED A VERY FAINT GRAY BLUE, AND COVERED WITH CLEAR GLAZE. A LOVELY PIECE.

WHITE IMPERIAL POTTERY WAS ONLY FOR MOURNING

ACQUIRED FROM HAZE MART, SEATTLE
8-24-43
ASPE

IN COLLECTION OF HENRY C. HITT

MADE OF PORCELAIN COLOR AS NOTED

WORKMANSHIP SO FINE THE ARTIST SIGNED IT. SIZE, mm 10+60 x 24 SQ. (4)

PROBABLE REIGN LATE K'ANG HSI DATES 1720 CIRCA (Note 1)

HAS ORIGINAL (2) SPOON-STOPPER OF GREEN JADE, AMBER SPOON

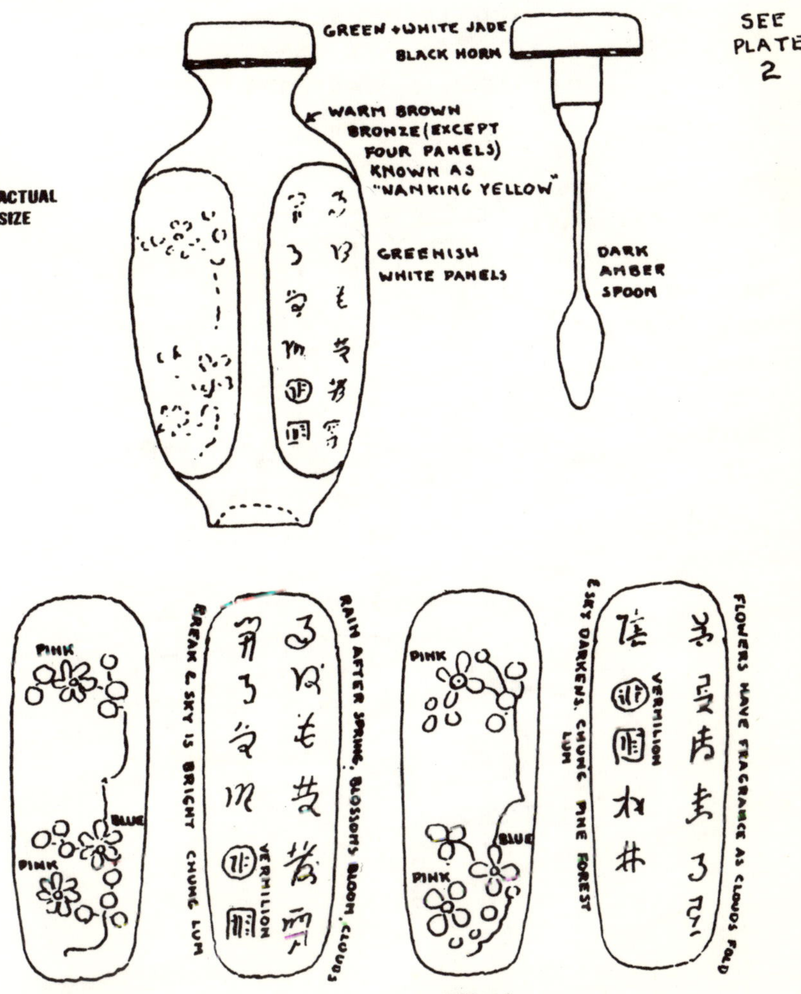

FLOWERS WITH YELLOW CENTERS, LEAVES ROUND IN VARYING GREENS.

SEE NOTE 13
LETTERING BLACK EXCEPT SIGNATURES.

ACQUIRED FROM H. SOOYSMITH

MADE OF PORCELAIN **COLOR** FAMILLE ROSE

WORKMANSHIP FINE, TRANSLUCENT PURE WHITE **SIZE, mm** 50+10×65×26 (4)

PROBABLE REIGN CH'IEN LUNG, AS MARKED **DATES** 1735-96 (Note 1)

HAS ORIGINAL (2) **SPOON-STOPPER OF** CORAL GLAZED WHITE PORCELAIN.

DESIGN IS LARGELY INCISED AND IS OUTLINED IN BLACK INK, COLORS ARE GLAZED. DETAIL FINE. CONDITION IS LIKE NEW.

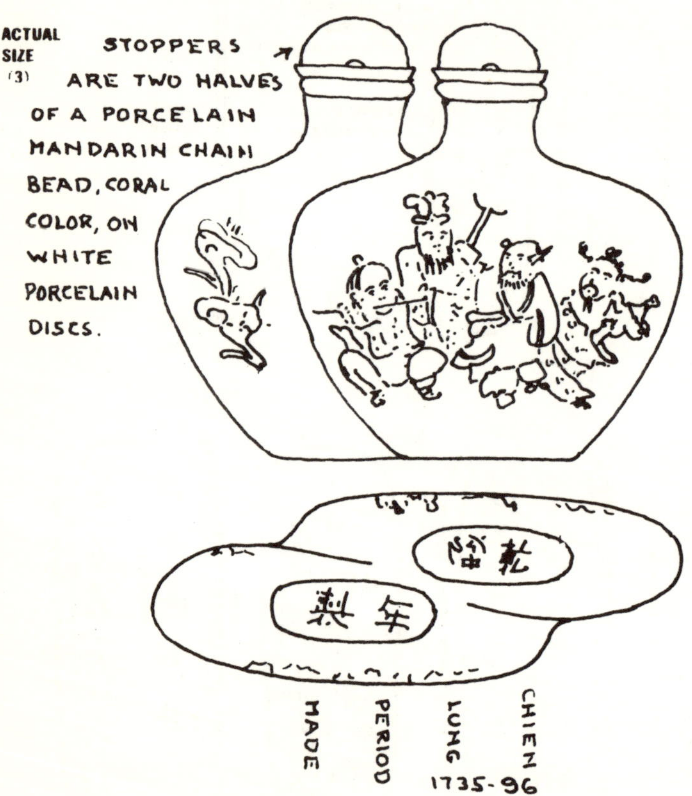

THE EIGHT TAOIST IMMORTALS

SEE OPPOSITE FOR 1½ SIZE DETAILS OF BOTH SIDES.

ACQUIRED FROM MR. ARTHUR LOVELESS
AAER 7-25-44

LÜ TUNG-PIN
THE ELDEST, A SCHOLAR, THE PATRON OF MAGICIANS & BARBERS. HAS MAGIC SWORD, EMBLEM OF CELESTIAL SERENITY.

LI TIEH-KUAI
THE IMMORTAL LAME BEGGAR, WITH CROOKED IRON STAFF & PILGRIM GOURD, EMBLEM OF NECROMANCY, SHOWN SMOKING.

HO HSIEN KO
IMMORTAL VIRGIN DAMSEL, WITH LOTUS FLOWER THE EMBLEM HERE OF FERTILITY.

LAN TS'AI-HO
WITH BASKET OF FRUIT OR FLOWERS, PIETISTIC, SUPERLATIVE. (SOMETIMES IS OLD MAN, OR A GIRL)

COLORS.
ROSE = R
YELLOW.Y
BLUE = B
TURQOISE.T
ORANGE O
VIOLET = V

DELICATE FLESH.

BLACK INK OUTLINES.

HAN HSIANG TU
THE IMMORTAL MUSICIAN, WITH HIS FLUTE, EMBLEMATIC OF SEAT OF LIFE AND INTELLECT.

CHANG KUO-LAO
WITH BAMBOO TUBE & RODS, EMBLEMATIC OF LONGEVITY AND PIOUS AFFECTION. (OFTEN ON DONKEY)

CHUNG-LI CHÜAN
WITH FAN, HAS POWER TO REVIVE SOULS OF DEAD. IS SHOWN BEARDED, CORPULENT, HALF NAKED.

TSAO KUO-CH'IN
WEARS OFFICIAL HAT AND FINE CLOTHES, OFTEN HAS CASTINETS EMBLEMATIC OF REVIVAL.

MADE OF PORCELAIN, WHITE, CRACKLED COLOR SEVEN COLOR DECORATION ON GLAZE (4)

WORKMANSHIP SUPERB. SIZE, mm 6+66 x 40 DIA.

PROBABLE REIGN CHIEN LUNG, DATED DATES 1735-1796 (Note 1)

HAS ORIGINAL (2) SPOON-STOPPER OF BLACK HORN

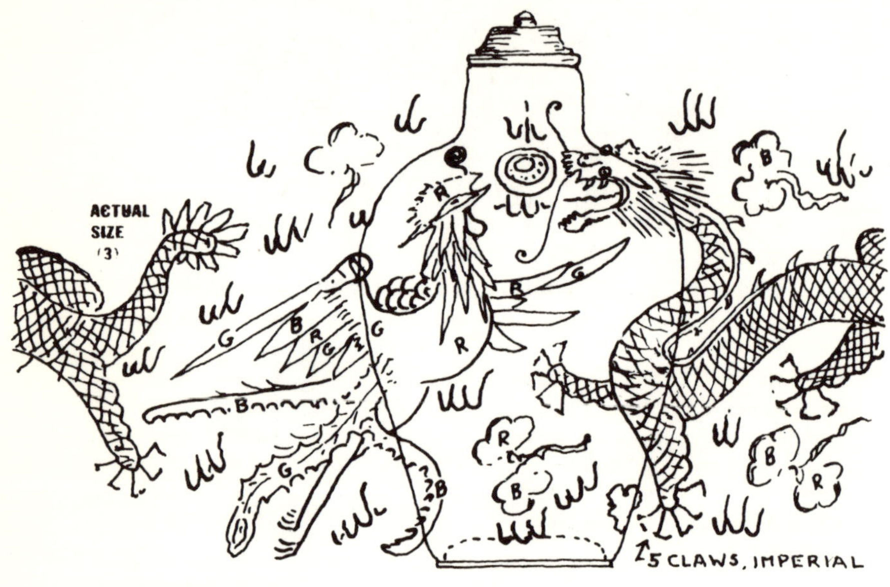

SEVEN COLORS OVER WHITE CRACKLE GLAZE ON WHITE BASE

VERMILION - ALL OF DRAGON & FLAMES W. PHOENIX LEGS, COMB, WATTLES

BLACK - DRAGON'S EYES, OUTLINE OF PHOENIX

BLUE GREEN - FLAMING PEARL

YELLOW - CLOUD STREAMERS.

ROSE - MARKED R
BLUE " B
GREEN " G

PERIOD 年乾 CHIEN
MADE 製隆 LUNG
1735 - 1796

A PHOENIX, SYMBOLIZING THE EMPRESS, AND DRAGON, THE EMPEROR, STRIVING AFTER THE FLAMING PEARL, PERFECTION, SURROUNDED BY FLAMES AND CLOUDS

ACQUIRED FROM MRS PARKS, SEATTLE, 6-7-44
KUEX

IN COLLECTION OF HENRY C. HITT

MADE OF PORCELAIN, WHITE, FAINT GREEN GL. **COLOR** BLUE, UNDER GLAZE

WORKMANSHIP FINE **SIZE, mm** **(4)**

PROBABLE REIGN YUNG CHÊNG . DATED **DATES** 1723-35 **(Note 1)**

HAS ORIGINAL (2) SPOON-STOPPER OF ? BONE

WAS PROBABLY NOT ORIGINALLY A SNUFF BOTTLE

ACTUAL SIZE (3)

SHAPE OF A BOTTLE GOURD (HO-LU) A TAOIST SYMBOL AND THE EMBLEM OF LI TIEH KUAI, SEE PAGE 63.

THIS GOURD IS KEPT IN HOMES TO WARD OFF EVIL.

SMALL ONES, BEAUTIFULLY DECORATED, ARE USED AS CAGES FOR FIGHTING AND SINGING CRICKETS.

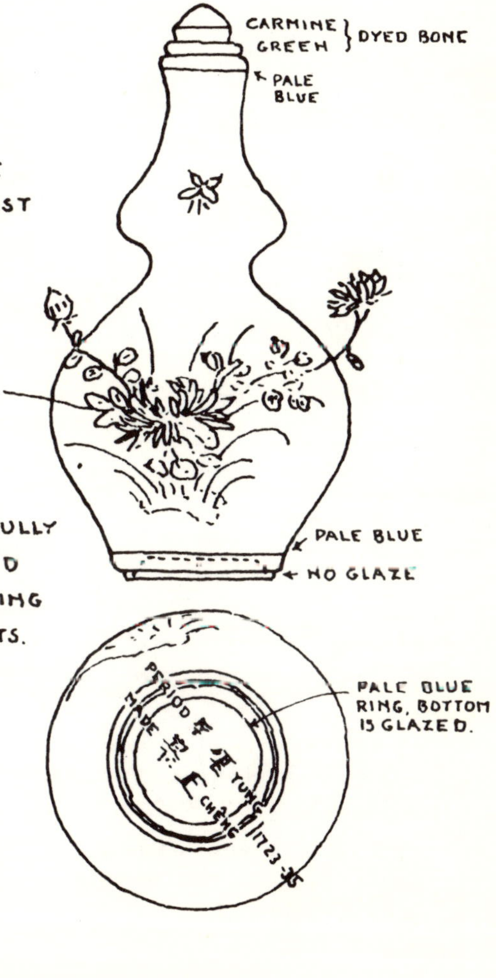

SEE PLATE 3

ACQUIRED FROM MRS. GERTRUDE STUART 10-1-44

SEE

IN COLLECTION OF HENRY C. HITT

MADE OF PORCELAIN, TRANSLUCENT **COLOR** YELLOW-CREAM GLAZE

WORKMANSHIP IMPERIAL POTTERY **SIZE, mm** 9+71x42x24 (4)

PROBABLE REIGN CH'IEN LUNG **DATES** 1735-1796 (Note 1)

HAS ORIGINAL (2) **SPOON-STOPPER OF** GREEN MALACHITE

ACTUAL SIZE (3)

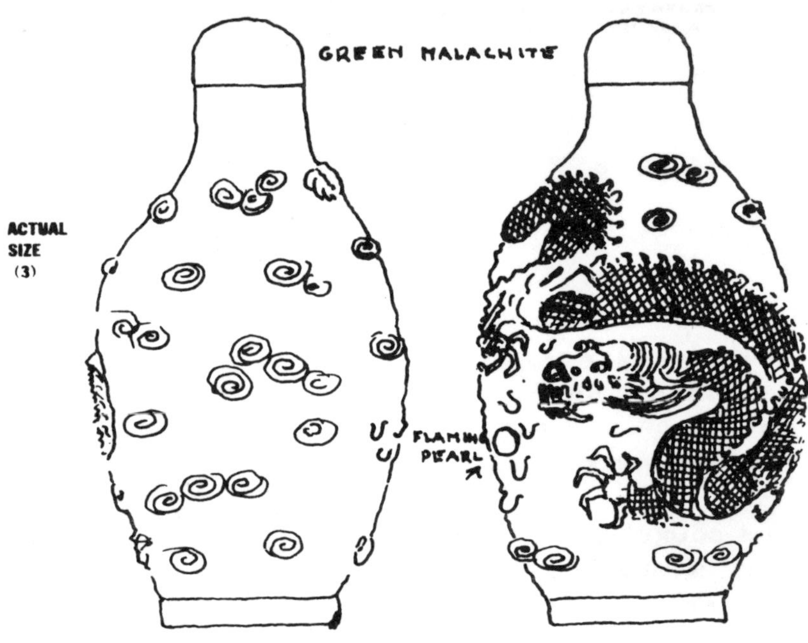

·ALL YELLOW-CREAM GLAZE EXCEPT MINUTE BLACK EYES, ON FINE WHITE TRANSLUCENT PORCELAIN BASE. DESIGN IS MINUTELY MODELLED AND CARVED, ADDED TO A PLAIN MOLDED PORCELAIN BOTTLE.

NO INSCRIPTION, OBVIOUSLY CH'IEN LUNG IMPERIAL POTTERY. WITH 5 CLAWED DRAGON.

YELLOW WAS THE IMPERIAL COLOR DURING THE MANCHU DYNASTY 1644-1912.

DRAGON'S HEAD STANDS OUT, STARTLINGLY LIFE LIKE, FULLY MODELLED IN PORCELAIN, BLACK EYES.

ACQUIRED FROM HAZE MART, SEATTLE
8-24-43
AFIX

IN COLLECTION OF HENRY C. HITT

MADE OF PORCELAIN, PAINTED UNDER GLAZE COLOR WHITE

WORKMANSHIP FINE FOR THE PERIOD* SIZE, mm 64+10×55×38 (4)

PROBABLE REIGN DATED T'UNG CHIH DATES 1862-74 (Note 1)

HAS ORIGINAL (2) SPOON-STOPPER OF WALRUS IVORY, DYED.

*R.L. HOBSON STATES THE T'UNG CHIH PERIOD SHOWS US CHINESE PORCELAIN AT ITS LOWEST EBB. THIS IS DELICATELY PAINTED.

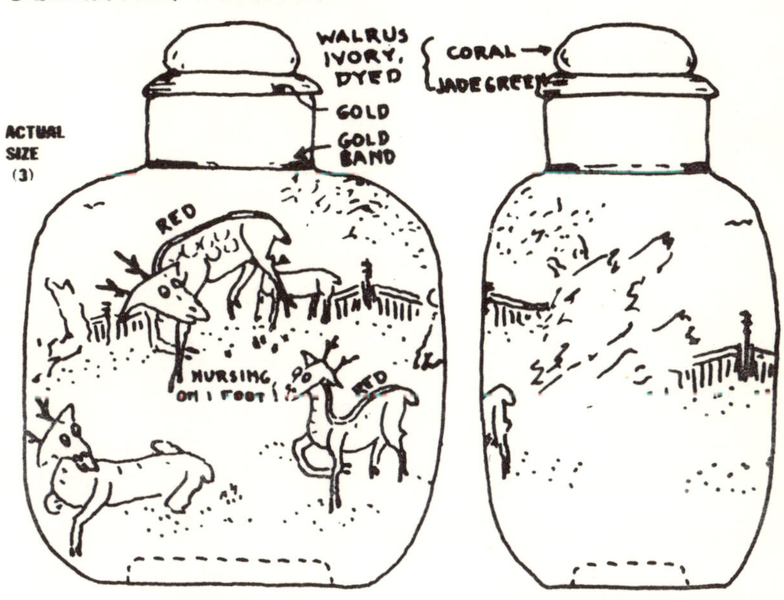

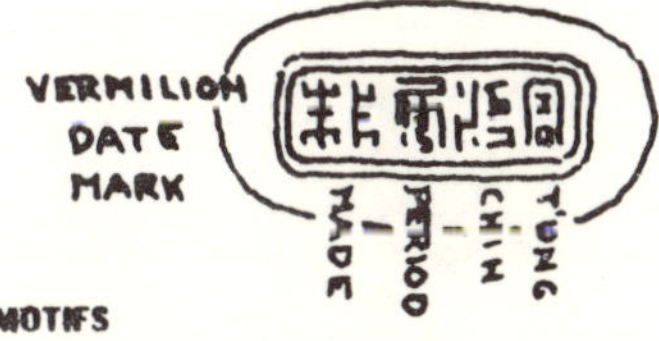

3 DEER + 1 FAWN ARE IRON RED (ROUGE DE FER), 2 DEER GRAY BLACK, GREEN GRASS, PINK ROCKS.

MOTIFS

OBVERSE SHOWS 3 MORE SIKA DEER PLUS A FAWN, ON ITS MOTHER'S BACK! AND WITH ANTLERS!

SIKA DEER (SPOTTED) OR "ROSE-FLOWER" DEER, IS SACRED, EMBLEM OF OFFICIAL AWARDS; RIDDEN BY SHAO SHING, GOD OF LONGEVITY, & KUAN YIN, GODDESS OF MERCY, AN INCARNATION OF BUDDHA

ACQUIRED FROM PRESENT FROM H. SOOYSMITH
5-10-43

68

MADE OF PORCELAIN COLOR GRAY WHITE

WORKMANSHIP FINE SHAPE, FAIR PAINTING SIZE, mm 67X37 DIA (4)

REIGN DATED HUNG HUEN DATES 1913-14 (Note 1)

HAS ORIGINAL (2) SPOON-STOPPER OF DYED BONE

ACTUAL SIZE

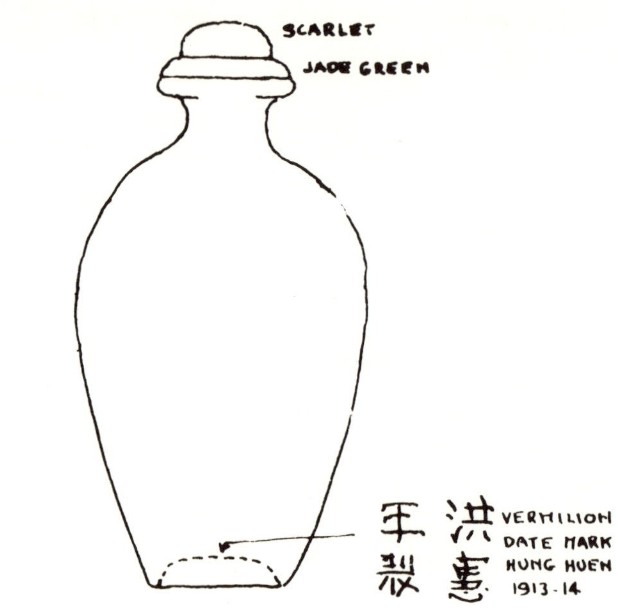

MOTIFS

FEAST OF LANTERNS, NEW YEARS

ACQUIRED FROM H. SOOYSMITH

IN COLLECTION OF HENRY C. HITT

MADE OF PORCELAIN, WHITE BASE COLOR BLACK

WORKMANSHIP FAIR, SEE BELOW SIZE, mm 71+6×36×19 (4)

PROBABLE REIGN TAO KUANG DATES 1821-50 (Note 1)

HAS ORIGINAL (2) SPOON-STOPPER OF ROSE QUARTZ

ACTUAL SIZE (3)

OTHER SIDE HAS SAME DESIGN

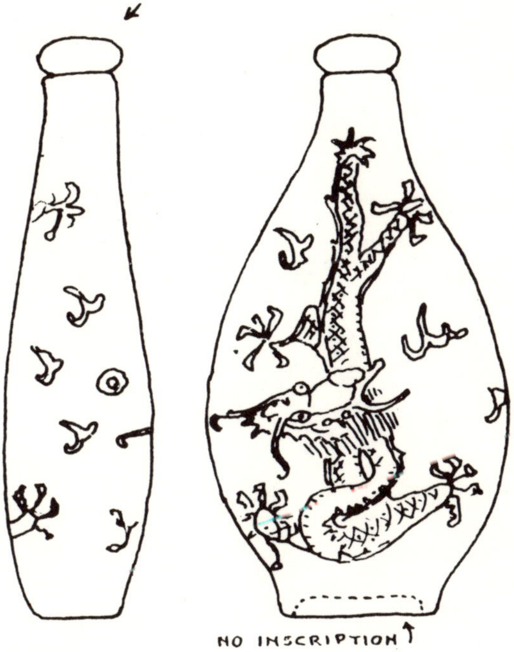

NO INSCRIPTION

DESIGN IS DRAWN IN BLACK. DRAGONS ARE TINTED YELLOW AND BLUE GREEN, FLAMES AND PEARLS ALSO BLUE GREEN.

REST OF BOTTLE, EXCEPT BOTTOM, IS COVERED WITH THICK COAL BLACK GLAZE; NEW IN TAO KUANG REIGN.

ACQUIRED FROM H. SOOYSMITH 7-17-44
RUEK

IN COLLECTION OF HENRY C. HITT

70

MADE OF PORCELAIN | COLOR WHITE

WORKMANSHIP FAIR | SIZE, mm 65+3×54×20 (4)

PROBABLE REIGN TAO KUANG | DATES 1831 (Note 1)

HAS (2) SPOON-STOPPER OF VERMILION BONE

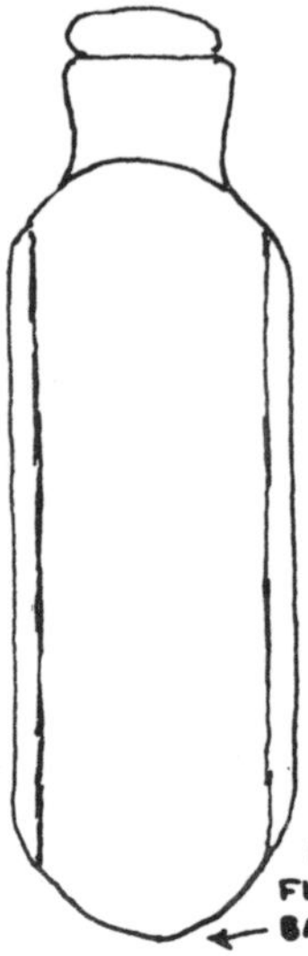

PHOENIX (8)
BLUE BODY
CARMINE HEAD
VERMILION FEET
" + BROWN TAIL

ACTUAL SIZE (3)

BLUE ROCKS, RED BERRIES

BROWN ROBE

NO FLAT BASE.

GOLD

CYCLICAL DATE
HSIN 辛
MAO 卯
= 28
= 1831
SEE NOTE

INSCRIPTION IS IN THE "TS'AO" OR CURSIVE FORM, ABBREVIATED & DISTORTED BUT USED FOR VITALITY AND FREEDOM

孝心能感格天意惜残生辛卯冬月步甫

PITYING / MAKE / RESPECTFUL
REAL / WILTED / HEART
GODS
LIVES / CAN
OPINION

NAME OF ARTIST

VERMILION SEAL

EARLY WINTER

INSCRIPTION IS IN BLACK.

ASER

IN COLLECTION OF H. SOOYSMITH

MADE OF **PORCELAIN** COLOR GRAY, BLUE DESIGN

WORKMANSHIP FINE SIZE, mm 8+76×45×25 (4)

PROBABLE REIGN DATES (Note 1)

HAS ORIGINAL (2) SPOON-STOPPER OF GLASS

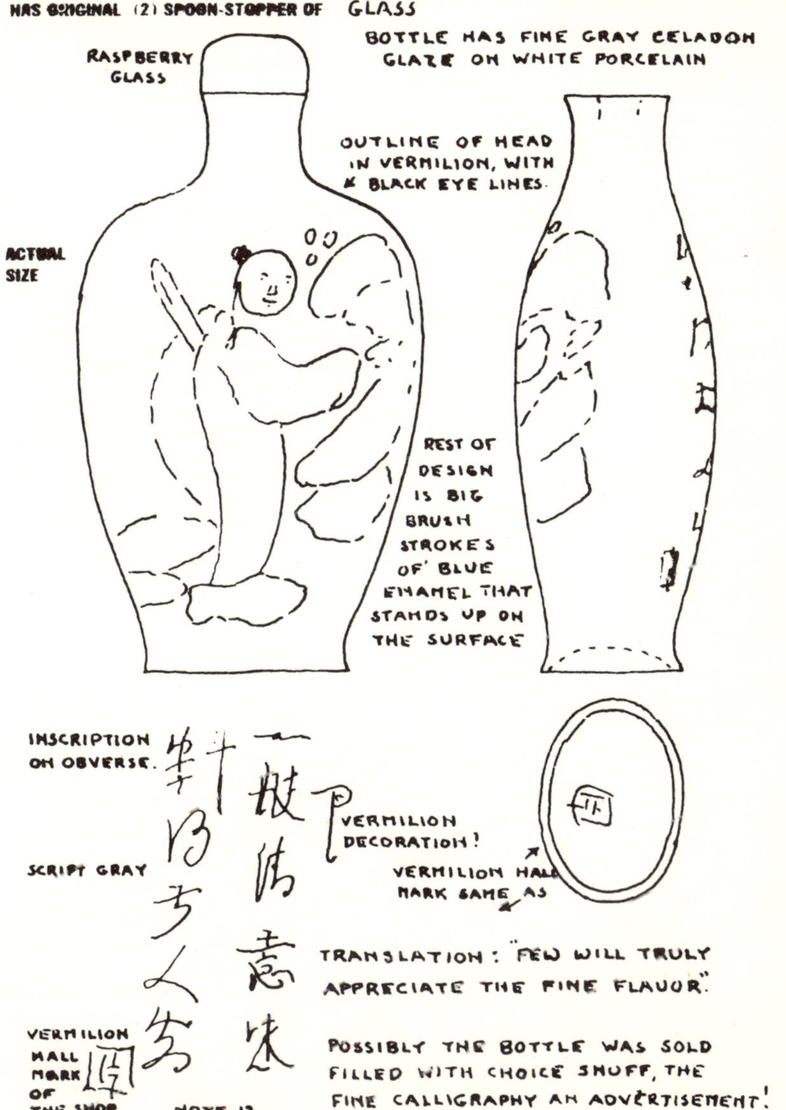

ACQUIRED FROM DOLLY MADISON, SEATTE
ESEG

IN COLLECTION OF HENRY C. HITT

MADE OF PORCELAIN **COLOR** GREEN GROUND

WORKMANSHIP FINE, LINES INDENTED **SIZE, mm** (4)

REIGN DATED CHIA CH'ING **DATES** 1796-1820 (Note 1)

HAS ORIGINAL (2) SPOON-STOPPER OF GLASS & IVORY

ACTUAL SIZE

DARK GREEN GROUND.

DESIGN VIOLET, PINK, GREEN

LINES INDENTED IN THE PORCELAIN

SHOU = IMMORTALITY, ONE OF MANY CONVENTIONAL FORMS. THE FLORAL DESIGN IS ANOTHER.

SEE OTHER PAGES FOR SCRIPT FORM AND OTHER CONVENTIONS. ONE ON TITLE PAGE.

HALF OF DESIGN, IT REPEATS.

MADE OF "PORCELAIN", "COARSELY MANUFACTURED" COLOR SEE BELOW

WORKMANSHIP "VERY INFERIOR" SIZE, ~~mm~~ 2" HIGH (4)

PROBABLE REIGN TAO KUANG 1821-50 DATES 1821-30 (Note 1)

HAS ORIGINAL (2) SPOON-STOPPER OF NONE. CALLED "EXACTLY IDENTICAL WITH SNUFF BOTTLES ACTUALLY ON THE MARKET IN CHINA" BY SIR JOHN FRANCIS DAVIS, "THE CHINESE", 1836.

ACTUAL SIZE (3)

TYPICAL, SOME ARE PLAIN WITHOUT GRAIN BORDER.

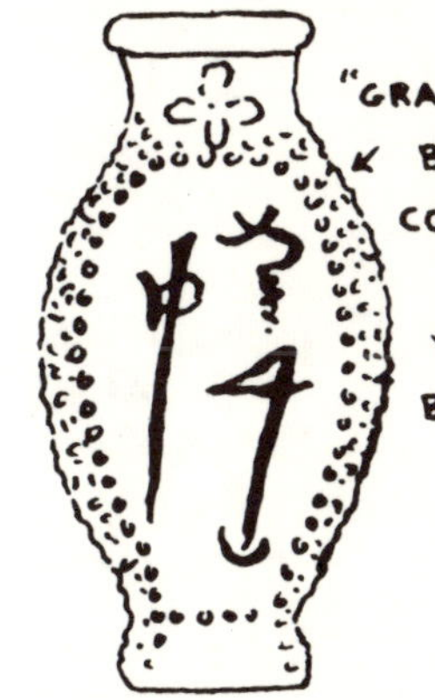

FOUND 100 YEARS AGO IN ANCIENT EGYPTIAN TOMBS.

BUT THEY MUST HAVE BEEN PLANTED BY THE ARAB WORKMEN TO FOOL THE ARCHEOLOGISTS!

REPORTED 1832 BY PROF. ROSELLINI AS FOUND BY HIM AND SEVERAL OTHERS IN THEBES TOMBS. 2000 B.C.
1837 BY SIR JOHN GARDNER WILKINSON.
1836 BY SIR JOHN FRANCIS DAVIS (SEE NOTE ↑)
1853 BY SIR AUSTIN H. LAYARD IN A TOMB AT NINEVEH, BUT HE WAS NOT FOOLED.

IN MUSEUMS: THE LOUVRE, BRITISH MUSEUM, THE ASHMOLEAN MUSEUM, ET CETERA.

IN COLLECTIONS: L'HOTE, ROBT. HAY, DUKE OF NORTHUMBERLAND, AND THE NEW YORK HISTORICAL SOCIETY ON LOAN IN THE BROOKLYN MUSEUM.

WERE FINALLY IDENTIFIED AS TAO KUANG BY R.L. HOBSON IN "CHINESE POTTERY & PORCELAIN", 1915.

DATA FROM "A TEMPEST IN A SNUFF BOTTLE" BY ELIZABETH RIEFSTAHL IN THE BROOKLYN MUSEUM QUARTERLY, APR. 1938.

74

MADE OF POTTERY

COLOR VARIOUS

WORKMANSHIP VERY INTERESTING GLAZES

SIZE, mm 8+69X63X30 (4)

PROBABLE REIGN CH'IEN LUNG (?)

DATES 1736-95 (Note 1)

HAS ORIGINAL (2) SPOON-STOPPER OF GLASS

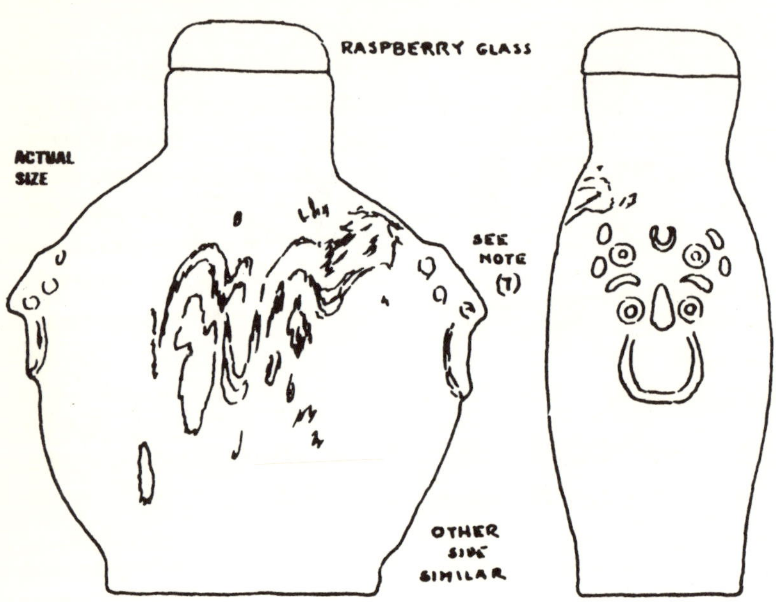

A VERY INTERESTING POTTERY STUDY. BISQUE IS LIGHT BROWN, CARVED WITH TIGER HEADS. DESIGN OF BLUE, BLACK, AND OPAQUE GLAZES WAS DRAGGED WHILE MELTED INTO INTERESTING PATTERNS. THE WHOLE WAS LATER COVERED WITH A CLEAR BLUE GLASS-LIKE CRACKLE GLAZE ALL OVER.

WHILE APPARENTLY NOT MARKED THIS IS VERY LIKE A BOTTLE SHOWN AS FIG. 74 IN "CHINESE ART" BY BUSHELL DESCRIBED AS SIGNED UNDER THE GLAZE BY KÜ YÜEH HSÜAN STUDIO NAME (CHAMBER OF THE ANCIENT MOON) OF HU, THE CELEBRATED DIRECTOR OF THE CHIEN LUNG IMPERIAL FACTORY.

ACQUIRED FROM DOLLY MADISON, SEATTLE

IN COLLECTION OF HENRY C. HITT

古月軒製

CHIA CH'ING BOTTLES IN HIGH RELIEF

Outstanding in every collection of snuff bottles, these are usually erroneously called carved porcelain. That they were formed in moulds in some complicated manner, with only minor touching up, is however evident from any study of duplicates. Though the design in some types is in two superimposed layers like some in this collection, the relation between these layers is found to be duplicated. The lower layer, in a rectangular diaper pattern, will have an arabesque surface design; and on top of this layer the motifs, such as dragon and phoenix, or buddhist emblems, will be found to be placed very nearly the same on duplicate bottles. Nearly every fine detail of both layers will be so closely duplicated as to prove some method of moulding was used.

A general similarity in shape, workmanship, and border motifs at top and base, and a thin wide lip, gold painted on top, indicates that they were all from one factory, and polychrome bottles are dated for the reign of Chia Ch'ing, 1796-1820, probably early, before the decadence.

There are 20 or more designs, and individual bottles in each design may be either all over glazed, in various colors, or enameled in polychrome. Those in monochrome were apparently dipped in colored glaze and this has usually chipped off the highest ridges of the intricate design so as to leave a spotted effect. The porcelain biscuit underneath is cream colored, a special mixture including soapstone which is incorrectly called "soft paste" from somewhat similar European porcelains. The Chinese porcelain of this type is hard and was probably used because it moulded better and stood up better in the kiln for these very delicate shapes than white porcelain paste. It is not tough, and these bottles are often found cleverly repaired. (see Pages 78 & 79) The Fuller Collection has one still in biscuit that has partially collapsed.

Apparently this beautiful technique in porcelain was used only for snuff bottles.

MADE IN
HAN DYNASTY
206 B.C. - 220 A.D.

JADE CAT WITH
TWO TAILS

ANCIENT
YAO PING OR
MEDICINE
BOTTLE
THAT WOULD
MAKE A
SNUFF
BOTTLE
2000 YRS.
OLD!

ACTUAL SIZE,
67 mm HIGH.

JADE, RUSSET
BROWN WITH
GRAY AND
BLACK MARKS.

IN COLLECTION
W. G. WRIGLEY.
ENGLAND

DATA FROM
"CHINESE JADE
THROUGHOUT
THE AGES"
P. 142 & PL. LXXV.

MADE OF PORCELAIN, CARVED SOFT PASTE **COLOR** COBALT BLUE GLAZE
WORKMANSHIP FINE, INTRICATELY CARVED & UNDERCUT **SIZE, mm** 73x40x28 (4)
PROBABLE REIGN CHIA CH'ING **DATES** 1796-1820 (Note 1)
SPOON-STOPPER OF GLASS

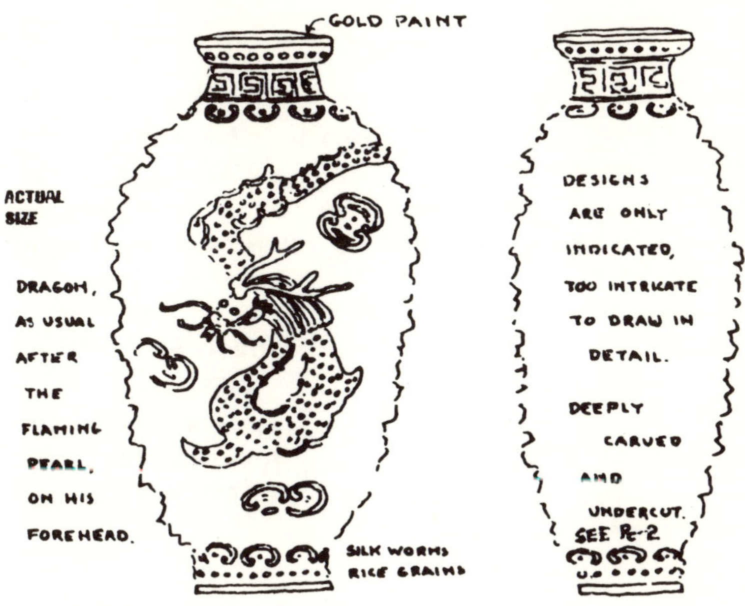

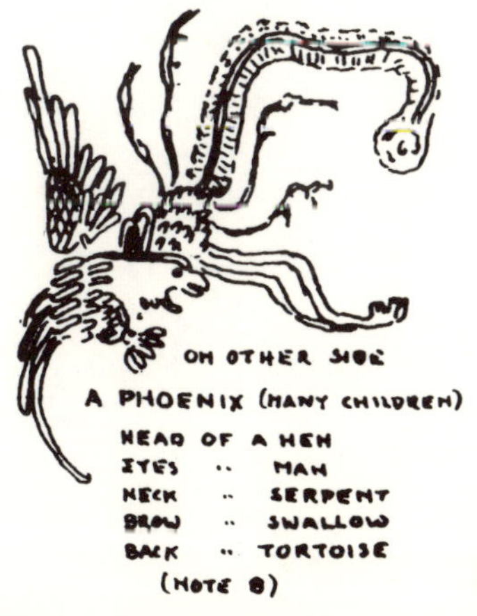

HAVE SEEN DUPLICATES OF THIS BOTTLE IN OTHER COLLECTIONS, WITH WHITE, TURQUOISE AND LIGHT BLUE GLAZES. THE SHAPE, THE GOLD ON THE TOP FACE, AND THE TOP & BOTTOM BORDERS ARE THE SAME AS THE PAGE 79 BOTTLE (DATED) & OTHERS WITH DIFFERENT DESIGNS.

MOTIF REPEATED 6 TIMES

ACQUIRED FROM H. SOOYSMITH
SLEG

IN COLLECTION OF HENRY C. HITT

78

MADE OF CARVED PORCELAIN **COLOR** CORAL GLAZE

WORKMANSHIP AS USUAL **SIZE, mm** 76+8×38×28 (4)

PROBABLE REIGN CHIA CH'ING **DATES** 1796-1820 (Note 1)

HAS ORIGINAL (2) SPOON-STOPPER OF SILVER MOUNTED PINK CRACKLE GLASS

ACTUAL SIZE (3)

A DISABLED VETERAN. NECK HAS BEEN REPLACED WITH SILVER AND BOTTOM REPAIRED WITH WHITE CEMENT. CORAL COLORED GLAZE LARGELY WORN OFF.

SHOWS LONG USE AND WAS TREASURED ENOUGH TO REPAIR.

THIS BOTTLE IS SIMILAR TO THE PRECEDING BOTTLE BUT IS FROM DIFFERENT MOLDS. THE OTHER IS THE TYPE FOUND IN MOST COLLECTIONS.

ACQUIRED FROM H. SOOYSMITH 7-17-44 UFEX

IN COLLECTION OF HENRY C. HITT

MADE OF PORCELAIN, CARVED SOFT PASTE · COLOR WHITE WITH COLORS

WORKMANSHIP EXQUISITE, DEEPLY UNDERCUT SIZE, mm 12+76×44×28 (4)

REIGN DATED CHIA CH'ING DATES 1796·1820 (Note 1)

HAS ORIGINAL (2) SPOON-STOPPER OF RED BEAD, IVORY, GREEN BONE

SEE PLATE 3

FOR DESIGNS SEE PAGE 33 AND 26.

ACTUAL SIZE

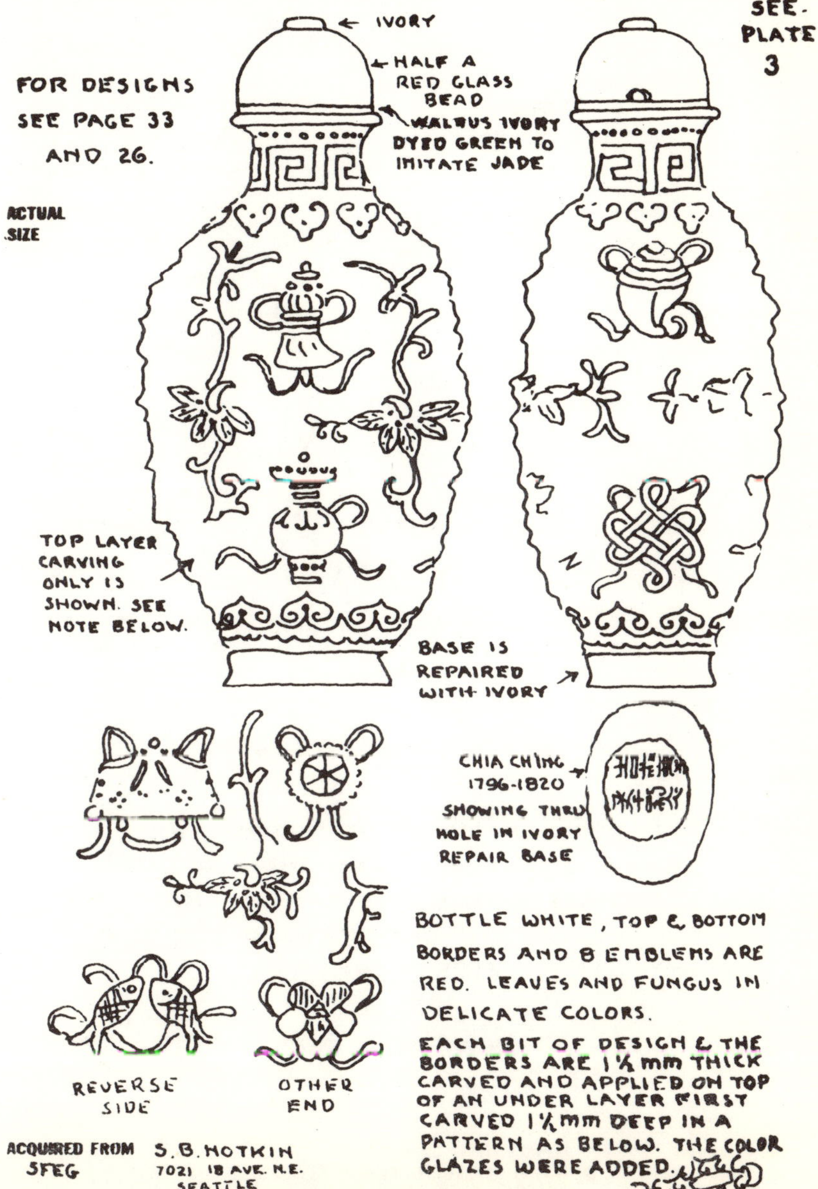

BOTTLE WHITE, TOP & BOTTOM BORDERS AND 8 EMBLEMS ARE RED. LEAVES AND FUNGUS IN DELICATE COLORS.

EACH BIT OF DESIGN & THE BORDERS ARE 1½ mm THICK CARVED AND APPLIED ON TOP OF AN UNDER LAYER FIRST CARVED 1½ mm DEEP IN A PATTERN AS BELOW. THE COLOR GLAZES WERE ADDED.

ACQUIRED FROM SFEG S. B. HOTKIN 7021 18 AVE. N.E. SEATTLE

IN COLLECTION OF HENRY C. HITT

MADE OF **PORCELAIN**, CARVED SOFT PASTE COLOR WHITE AND MANY COLORS

WORKMANSHIP NOT AS FINE AS SOME SIZE, mm 7+75 x 51 x 33 (4)

PROBABLE REIGN DATED CH'IEN LUNG DATES 1736-95 (Note 1)

HAS ORIGINAL (2) SPOON-STOPPER OF HALF A RED GLASS BEAD

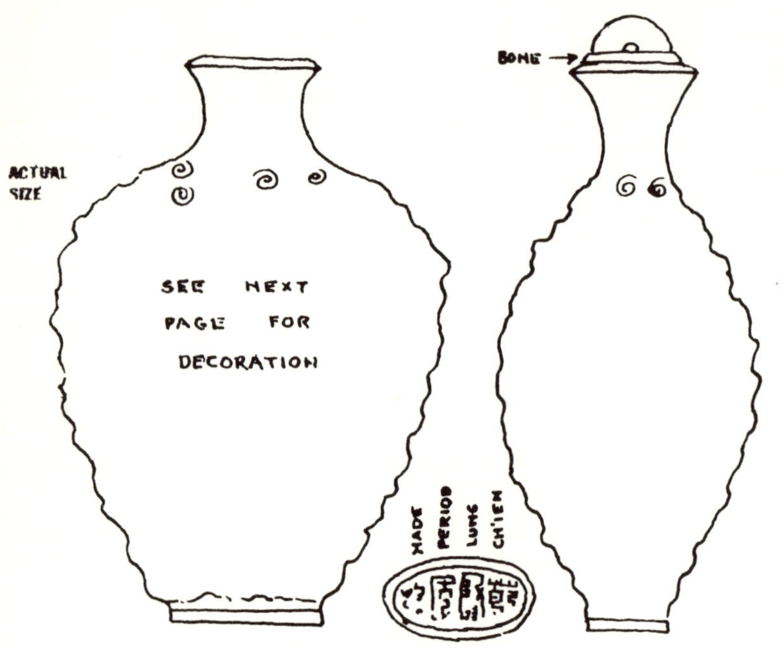

THE EIGHTEEN ARHAT

FAMOUS DISCIPLES OF BUDDHA, WHO CROSSED THE SEA FROM INDIA TO CHINA. DESIGN SHOWS THE SAINTS HAVE OVERCOME THE DANGERS OF THE SEA AND TAMED FIERCE ANIMALS.

SEE OPPOSITE PAGE

ACQUIRED FROM DOLLY MADISON, SEATTLE.
WAS COVERED WITH BROWN VARNISH!

IN COLLECTION OF HENRY C. HITT

1. THE ARHAT BHADRA (THE GOOD ONE) RIDING A TIGER AMONG THE CLOUDS.
2. JOYFULLY TOSSES HIS HAT IN THE AIR.
3. TWO COVER THEIR EARS TO KEEP OUT THE SOUND OF THE WILD WAVES.
4. CARRIES A PAGODA, HIS SYMBOL.
5. RATTLE STAFF THAT MONKS USE TO ATTRACT ATTENTION TO GET ALMS.
6. CARRYING YOUNG LION (?)
7. THIS SAINT USES A STAFF.
8. TWO WITH ALMS BOWLS.
9. PRAYING WITH FOLDED HANDS, A CUSTOM THAT ORIGINATED IN INDIA.

ALL BRIGHT COLORED

THE CARVED FACES ARE EXPRESSIVE, EYES PAINTED.

PLATE 3. See Pages 65,79.83,85,87.88.94

MADE OF CLOISONNE COLOR LAPIS BLUE

WORKMANSHIP CORRECT FOR ↙ SIZE, mm 75+10 X 38 DIA. (4)

PROBABLE REIGN K'ANG HSI OR EARLIER DATES 1662 - 1722 (Note 1)

BOTTLE MADE OF COPPER. NO TRACE OF GILDING.

SOLID LINES IN SKETCH INDICATE 357 CLOISONS OF COPPER, EACH 0.2 mm THICK. DOTTED LINES SHOW COLOR CHANGE WITHOUT CLOISONS.

ACTUAL SIZE (3)

FLOWERS (SINGLE MUMS ?) ARE BLUE, WHITE, PINK, YELLOW, MAROON. LEAVES GREEN & YELLOW.

WALRUS IVORY STAINED JADE

MAGPIES, BIRDS OF JOY, BLACK, WHITE YELLOW, BLUE

SEE PL. 3 ←

INDICATIONS BOTTLE DATES KANG HSI OR EARLIER :-

1. NOT ORIGINALLY FOR SNUFF, CONVERTED LIKE EARLY PORCELAIN BOTTLES.

2. LAPIS LAZULI BLUE GROUND, TYPICAL OF MING OR K'ANG HSI.

3. ENAMEL PITTED, A TROUBLE CURED ON CH'IEN LUNG CLOISONNE.

ACQUIRED FROM A. LOVEESS ILER

IN COLLECTION OF HENRY D. HITT

CLOISONNE

Cloisonne enamel originated in ancient Gaul, and was first made in China during the reign of Chih Cheng, 1341-67. Its popularity reached a peak during the later Ming Dynasty. A dark blue ground of powdered lapis lazuli and pitting of the enamel is typical of Ming or Kang Hsi cloisonne.

The cloisons, usually of copper, sometimes varied in thickness. They were delicately bent and cut to shape and fastened to the copper base with a vegetable glue from orchid roots until secured with powdered solder or enamel. The enamel was ground fine, packed in the spaces between the cloisons and fired, often three or four times. Finally the whole outside surface was ground flush, and often the edges of the cloisons were gilded. Cloisonne snuff bottles are rare, probably because cloisonne on copper is easily damaged by knocks.

1644, EARLIEST RECORDED SNUFF BOTTLE

Most snuff bottles, unless converted to snuff from some earlier use, date from the great reign of Ch'ien Lung, 1736-95. (See P. 60 for a Ming porcelain vase so converted dated the reign of Wan Li, 1573-1619; and P. 83 preceding for a similar cloisonne vase probably Kang Hsi, 1622-1722, or earlier.) But see opposite for one of a series of brass snuff bottles dated by one Cheng Wang Chang in 1644 to 1653 (the very beginning of the introduction of snuff in China) and authenticated by the Field Museum in Chicago.

MADE OF BRASS COLOR BRASS

WORKMANSHIP CAST, & ENGRAVED SIZE, mm 9+55x48x21 (4)

REIGN MARKED SHUN CHIH, 9TH YR. DATES 1651 (Note 1)

HAS (2) SPOON-STOPPER OF GLASS

CAST IN TWO HALVES AND SOLDERED ON THIS LINE

DESIGN IS ALL ENGRAVED.

ACTUAL SIZE (3)

DRAGONS RISING OUT OF THE SEA THRU THE CLOUDS CHASING THE FLAMING PEARL, SYMBOL OF MAN'S STRIVING FOR THE UN-ATTAIN-ABLE

DARK GREEN AND BLACK GLASS

FLAMES

SEE PL. 3.

CLOUDS

FLAMING PEARL

SEA

DRAGONS ARE 4 CLAWED, 5 WOULD BE ROYAL USE.

CHANG SHENG 9TH SHUN 1644-61 CHIH MADE WANG YR.

FLAMING PEARL

SAUCER 2MM DEEP

SEE NOTE P. 93.

TWO DRAGONS

"CHENG WANG CHANG MADE IN THE 9TH YEAR OF SHUN CHIH REIGN" 1651 A.D.

THE FIELD MUSEUM, CHICAGO, HAS A CLOSE DUPLICATE OF THIS, DATED 11TH YR., 1653, A DONATION FROM P. J. BAHR OF SHANGHAI, WHICH IS PICTURED AND ACCLAIMED AS UNIQUE IN ANTHROPOLOGY LFLT. 18.

H. SOOYSMITH HAS ANOTHER, SMALLER, 7+55x38x21, WITH THE SAUCER AND DRAGONS BOTH SIDES, DATED 1ST. YR. 1644

VERY EARLY DATES FOR SNUFF BOTTLES; BUT THEY APPEAR OLD; ARE CALLED AUTHENTIC BY THE FIELD MUSEUM; WERE DUPLICATED AT LEAST 1644-53; AND ARE INDESTRUCTIBLE.

ALBERT M. PYKE HAS DITTO, 1ST. YR., 9+56x47x21

ACQUIRED FROM H. SOOYSMITH 6-8-43 GLEX

MADE OF METAL, TUTENAG (12) COLOR DARK GRAY & GEMS

WORKMANSHIP FINE & PUZZLING SIZE, mm 10+80×45×23 (4)

PROBABLE REIGN MODERN

HAS ORIGINAL (2) SPOON-STOPPER OF SAME, LONG TIN SPOON

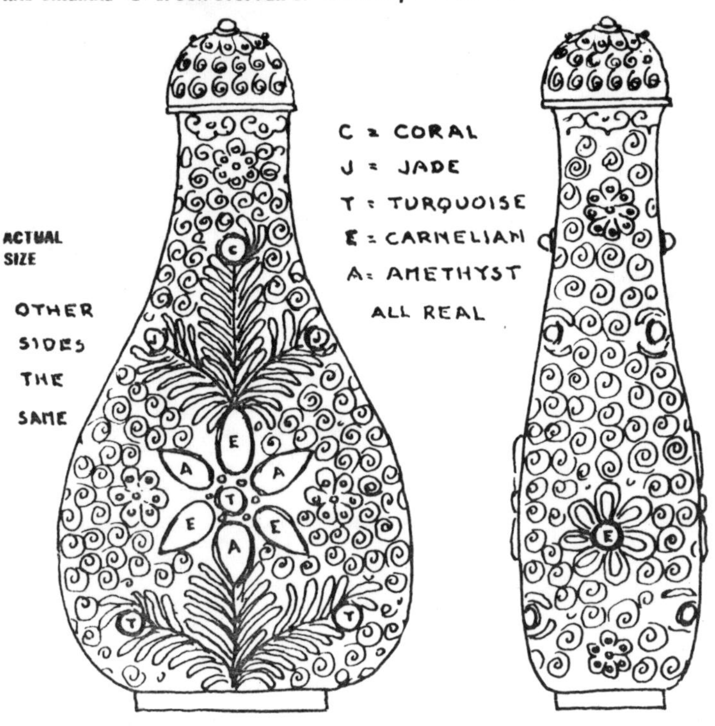

IT IS A PUZZLE HOW THIS BOTTLE, AND THAT ON P.87, WERE MADE. THEY ARE VERY LIGHT, VERY THIN TUTENAG PROBABLY CAST IN HALVES. THE LINES OF THE DECORATION ARE ALL TWISTED PAIRS OF VERY FINE WIRE, POSSIBLY ATTACHED WITH LACQUER AS NO TRACE OF SOLDER IS TO BE FOUND. THERE IS NO TRACE OF ROUGHNESS OR LOOSE WIRE ENDS. TINY BEADS AND THE JEWEL MOUNTINGS ARE LIKEWISE ATTACHED MOST MYSTERIOUSLY.

ACQUIRED FROM TATE HENRY, OLYMPIA, WN. ROGERS

IN COLLECTION OF HENRY C. HITT

MADE OF **METAL**, TUTENAG (12) COLOR WHITE PANELS ON GRAY

WORKMANSHIP FINE & PUZZLING SIZE, mm 10+77x45x34 (4)

PROBABLE REIGN MODERN ("CHINA CAST IN) DATES (Note 1)

HAS ORIGINAL (2) SPOON-STOPPER OF SAME LONG METAL SPOON

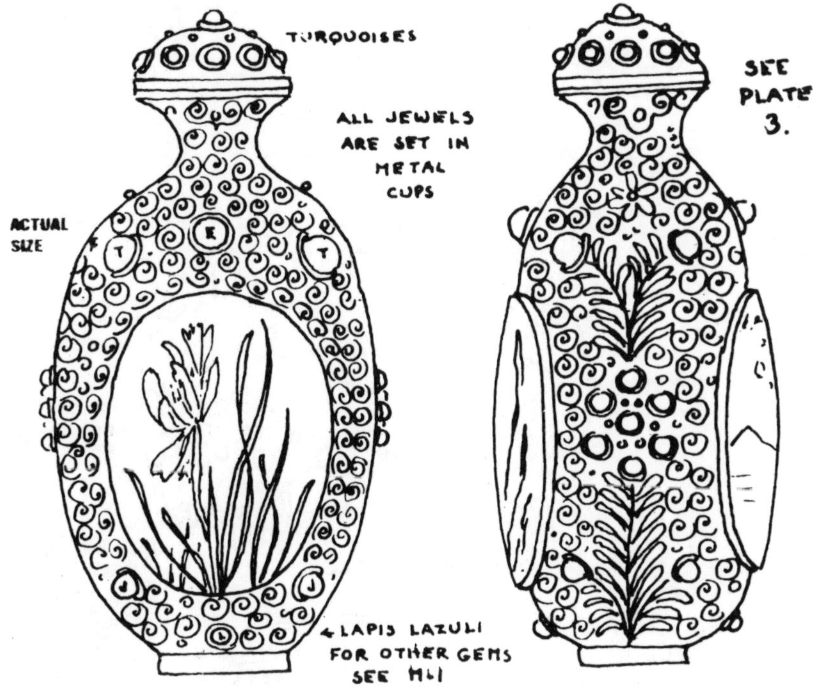

TURQUOISES

ALL JEWELS ARE SET IN METAL CUPS

SEE PLATE 3.

ACTUAL SIZE

← LAPIS LAZULI FOR OTHER GEMS SEE H-1

ENGRAVINGS ON CURVED PLATES OF POLISHED CREAM COLOR PLASTIC (?)

THE TINY BITS OF TWISTED WIRE ARE ONLY INDICATED HERE AND ON H-1. THERE ARE OVER 500 PIECES ON THIS BOTTLE, WITH NEVER A ROUGH END OR A TRACE OF SOLDER. IT IS POSSIBLE THAT THEY WERE MODELLED IN WAX AND THEN CAST BY THE PROCESS DENTISTS AND JEWELERS USE.

ACQUIRED FROM PRESENT FROM A KIND MOTHER-IN-LAW.

MADE OF METAL, TUTENAG (12) COLOR SILVER & ENAMELS

WORKMANSHIP CURIOUS SIZE, mm 9+67x60x30 (4)

PROBABLE REIGN MANCHURIAN DATES MODERN (Note 1)

HAS ORIGINAL (2) SPOON-STOPPER OF SAME

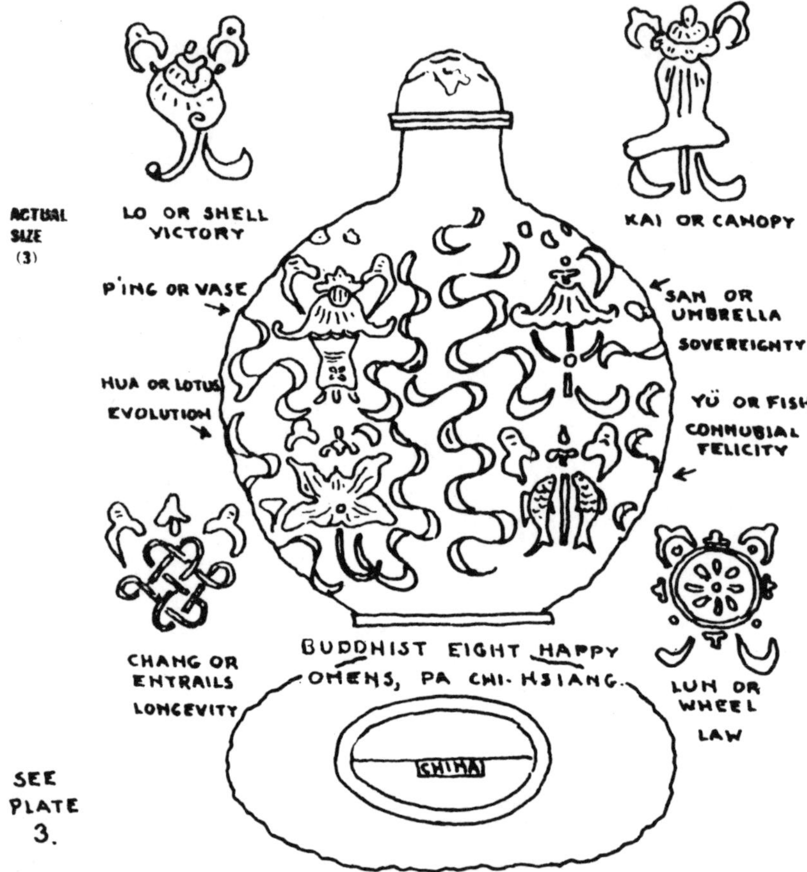

ALL THE DESIGN IS GAYLY LACQUERED IN TRANSPARENT LAPIS BLUE, LIGHT BLUE, AND MAROON ON AN OXIDIZED SILVER GROUND.

THE WHOLE BOTTLE APPEARS TO BE HAND HAMMERED AND CARVED. THE DESIGN, LACQUERED, STANDS OUT SHARPLY; THE GROUND IS FINE STIPPLE HAMMERED ALL OVER. IT WAS PROBABLY CAST IN SOME WAY. CURIOUS!

ACQUIRED FROM MRS. GERTRUDE STUART 10-1-44
NOF

IN COLLECTION OF HENRY C. HITT

MADE OF **MOTHER OF PEARL** COLOR PEARL, PAINTED

WORKMANSHIP GOOD SIZE, mm 2+60×35×12 (4)

PROBABLE REIGN ? DATES (Note 1)

HAS ORIGINAL (2) SPOON-STOPPER OF SAME

ACTUAL SIZE

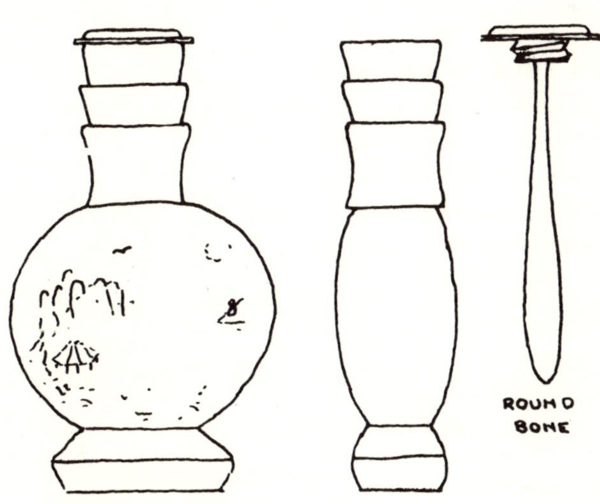

BRIGHTLY COLORED PAINTINGS ON BOTH SIDES, NEARLY ERASED.

NOT A SNUFF BOTTLE BUT AN UNUSUAL EXAMPLE OF A MOTHER OF PEARL BOTTLE WITH PAINTINGS.

ACQUIRED FROM CHINATOWN, VICTORIA, B.C.

IN COLLECTION OF HENRY C. HITT

MADE OF CINNABAR LACQUER, CARVED COLOR PURE VERMILION

WORKMANSHIP VERY FINELY CARVED SIZE, mm 12+72x64x28 (4)

PROBABLE REIGN CH'IEN LUNG ? DATES (Note 1)

HAS ORIGINAL (2) SPOON-STOPPER OF GLASS

ACTUAL SIZE

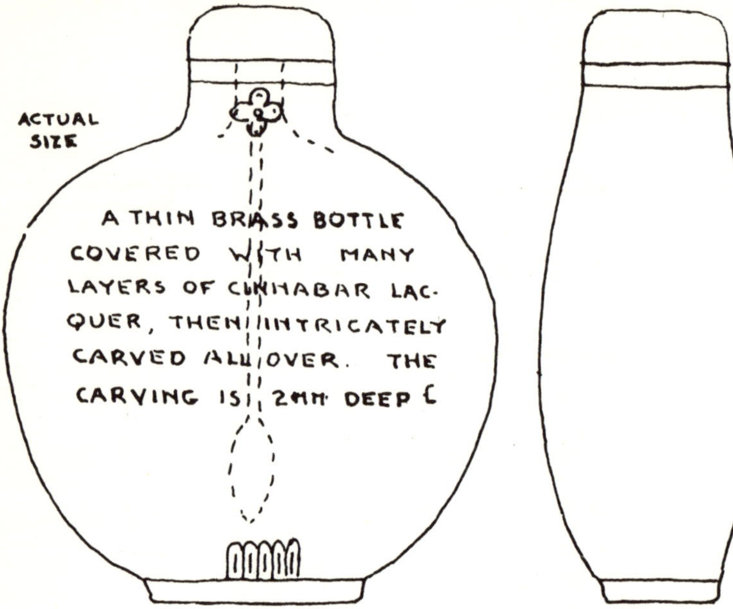

A THIN BRASS BOTTLE COVERED WITH MANY LAYERS OF CINNABAR LACQUER, THEN INTRICATELY CARVED ALL OVER. THE CARVING IS 2MM DEEP.

DESIGN IS THE SAME ON BOTH SIDES.

← LING CHIH, TAOIST FUNGUS OF IMMORTALITY, REVERED FOR 2000 YRS.

MOTIFS ARE ONLY INDICATED. DESIGN TOO INTRICATE AND DELICATELY CARVED TO DRAW IN DETAIL.

MAGPIES, SIGNIFY GOOD LUCK

PRUNE BLOSSOMS LONG LIFE

THE DESIGN WISHES THE OWNER A LONG LIFE & GOOD LUCK.

ACQUIRED FROM TATE HENRY, OLYMPIA ROGERS

IN COLLECTION OF HENRY C. HITT

STOPPERS & SPOONS

Many of the stoppers of Chinese snuff bottles with their tiny spoons are lovely OBJETS DE ART in themselves.

THE TWO BELOW ARE $1\frac{1}{2}$ FULL SIZE.

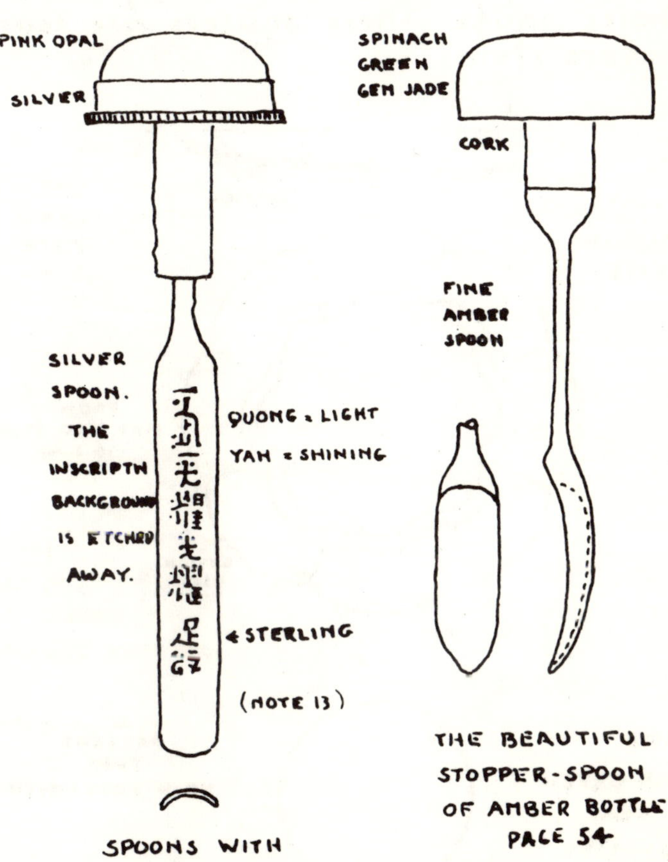

SPOONS WITH OWNERS NAMES ARE MUCH SOUGHT COLLECTORS PRIZES.

SNUFF SAUCERS

Snuff is believed in China to be beneficial to the health. as it was when first introduced with other tobacco in Europe.

So a considerate host at the end of a banquet passed around tiny saucers of choice snuff. These saucers are scarce collectors items.

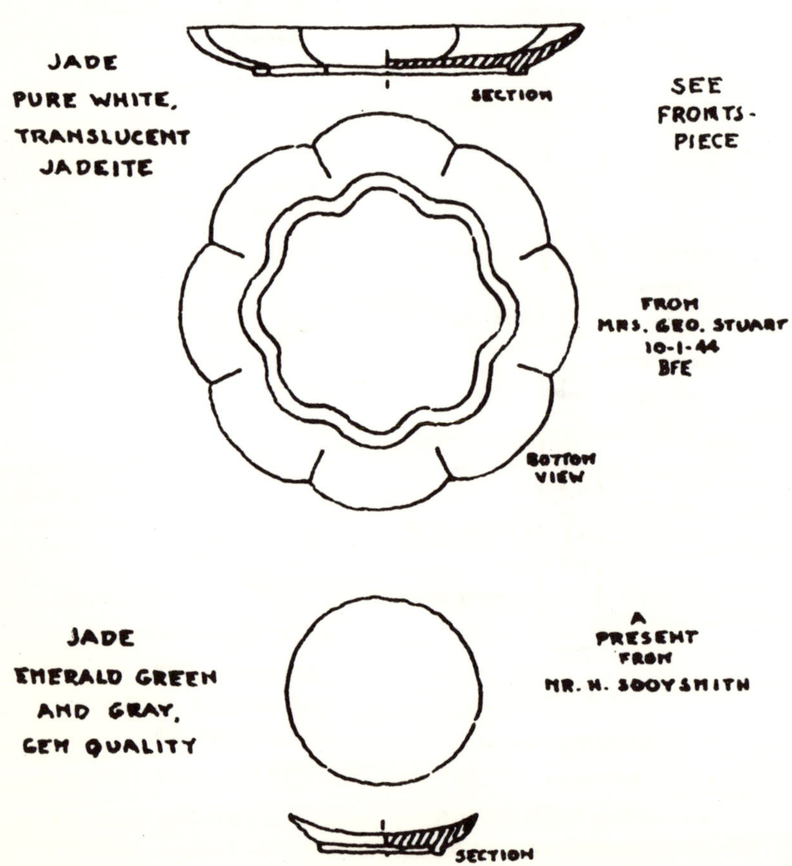

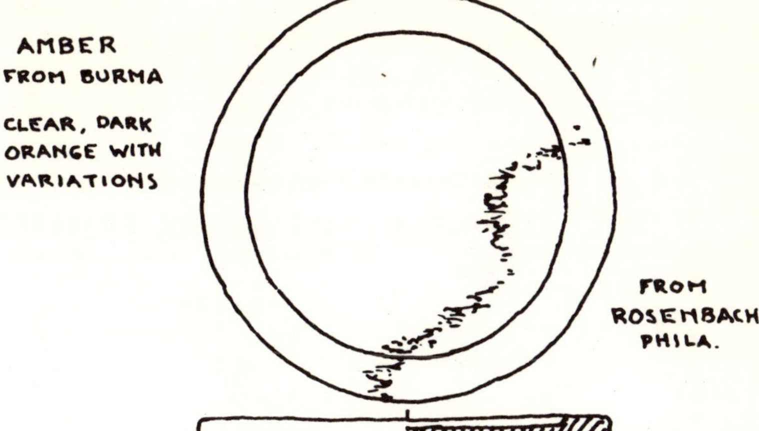

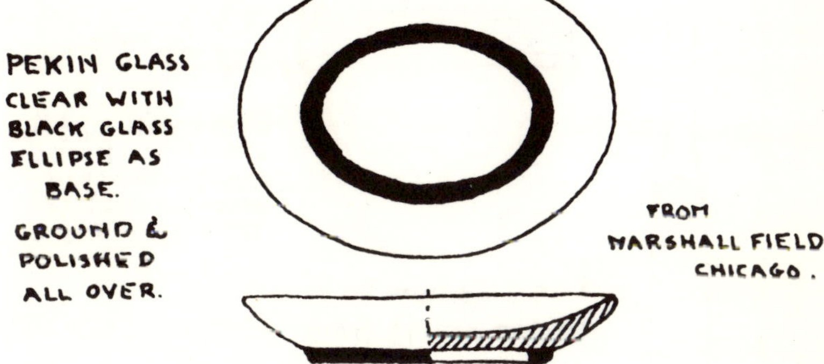

SEE PAGE 85
FOR SAUCERS ON
SIDES OF BOTTLES.

SNUFF SAUCERS WERE ALSO USED TO MIX PELLETS OF SNUFF AND WATER OR WINE TO PLACE BACK OF THE LIPS. THIS EXPLAINS THE SAUCER ON THE SIDE OF THE 1651 BOTTLE ON PAGE 85.

VERY OLD IVORY FUNNEL AND SPOON FOR FILLING SNUFF BOTTLES

SPOON 236 mm (9 INCHES) LONG.

The Spoon rich old ivory color

Funnel stained pinkish from snuff.

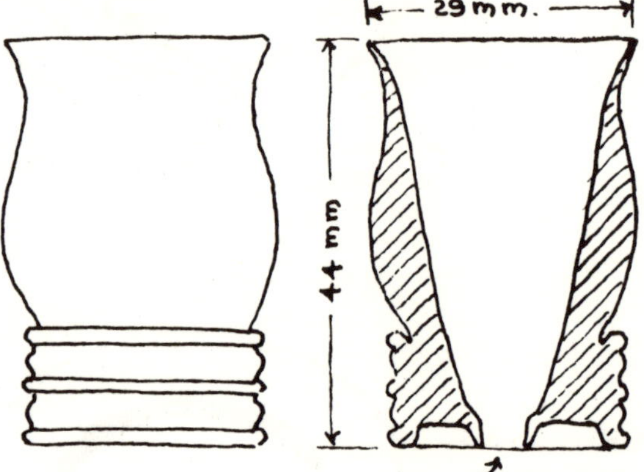

6 mm. dia. to fit small necks of snuff bottles, the funnel set on their tops.

Long spoon to ladle snuff from supply bottle to the Funnel.

Other end is a poker to work snuff down into the snuff bottle.

SEE PLATE 3.

FROM GUMPS, S.F.

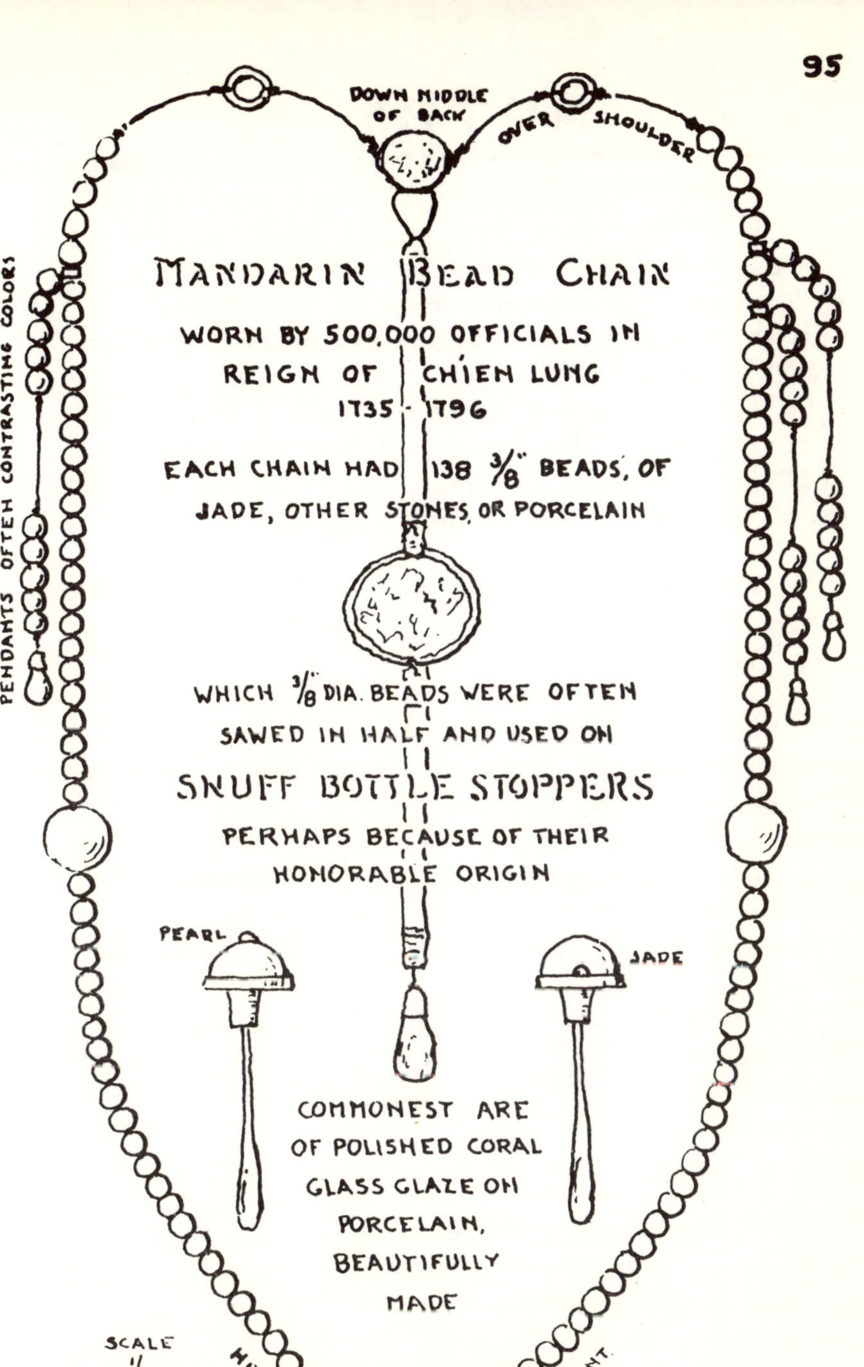
DOWN MIDDLE OF BACK
OVER SHOULDER
PENDANTS OFTEN CONTRASTING COLORS
MANDARIN BEAD CHAIN
WORN BY 500,000 OFFICIALS IN REIGN OF CHIEN LUNG 1735 - 1796
EACH CHAIN HAD 138 3/8" BEADS, OF JADE, OTHER STONES OR PORCELAIN
WHICH 3/8" DIA. BEADS WERE OFTEN SAWED IN HALF AND USED ON
SNUFF BOTTLE STOPPERS
PERHAPS BECAUSE OF THEIR HONORABLE ORIGIN
PEARL
JADE
COMMONEST ARE OF POLISHED CORAL GLASS GLAZE ON PORCELAIN, BEAUTIFULLY MADE
SCALE 1/3 SIZE
HUNG BELOW WAIST IN FRONT

NOTES

AS NUMBERED ON REFERENCES THRUOUT THE BOOK.

1. DATES. Very few snuff bottles bear a date, and dates when found may be quite erroneous. Workmanship is, however, a reliable guide for approximately fixing dates. If a bottle has been made with infinite patience and artistry it probably was made in the reign of CH'IEN LUNG in 1736-95, as all Chinese craftwork deteriorated after this. See Page 3.

2. Many stoppers did not originally belong to the bottles in which they now are found.

3. The drawings show the outline of the interior of bottles that were made by grinding by a dotted line --------. The hollowing out of these bottles by grinding was a very difficult feat and the value of a bottle depends largely on how thoroughly it was done. See Note 5 below.

4. Sizes are in millimeters: height of stopper + height of bottle x width x thickness. Many bottles have delicately carved wooden stands, and some will not stand up without a stand.

5. Bottles with only a drilled hole to house a fake spoon are marked "SEE NOTE 5" for a date when their workmanship indicates they belong to the Ch'ien Lung reign. See discussion of this matter on Page 5.

NOTES (CONTINUED)

6. In Chinese one sound often expresses several quite different written characters and frequently a design is a rebus based on some such a homophone; as it would be if we showed a BAT, the animal, to express "going on a bat, getting drunk.

In Chinese:

A BAT is a symbol of	HAPPINESS	(fu)
Color RED " " "	VAST	(hung)
A CARP FISH " " "	ABUNDANCE	
A GOAT " " "	PROSPERITY	

7. Many bottles are decorated only, on each lateral shoulder, with a very much conventionalized TIGER-HEAD holding a ring in its jaw. This design dates back to the Early Han Dynasty (206 B.C.-26 A.D.) when it was copied from actual handles on earlier bronze vessels.

8. The fabulous Chinese bird design usually called a PHOENIX is, according to Sowerby, not at all the phoenix of Egypt but two birds, FÊNG HUANG, fêng male, and huang female, of very good omen, appearing only at very long intervals when they portend some great and felicitous event.

FÊNG HUANG is the king of birds, the essence of the Yang principle. It has a hen's head, eyes of a man, neck of a serpent, locust's viscera, swallow's brow, and a fish's tail but with 12 or 13 feathers.

PINE. STRENGTH

9. The designs usually

called "hydras" are really conventionalized domestic cats, according to Sowerby.

10. A **DRAGON** is a truly marvellous beast with the head of a camel, horns of a deer, eyes of a rabbit, ears of a cow, neck of a snake, belly of a frog, scales of a carp, claws of a hawk, and palms of a tiger. It has whiskers and a beard. For Imperial use the feet have five claws, otherwise four. On its forehead or beard may appear a "night shining pearl" but he is more usually shown pursuing it, symbolical of us all striving for unattainable things. A dragon is a benevolent creature, controller of rain, and the Imperial emblem.

11. See Page 85 for bottles dated 1644 to 1653 that are obviously made for snuff and are apparently authentically dated. (The Field Museum records their 1653 bottle as made by Cheng Tsung Chang. It is believed this should read Cheng Wang Chang.)

12. Tutenag, tutenague, tootnague, tootnagle, or paktong is an alloy of zinc, copper, nickel, and iron peculiar to China.

13. Beautiful calligraphy (writing) is the very essence of Chinese art. Every character is a deep study in composition, balance, flow of line, and perfection in brush work. The copying in this book are sorry attempts.

14. This collection includes a wedge of dark green jade from upper British

NOTES (CONTINUED)

Columbia which was cut off a larger piece by ancient Indians using sand and sharp edged stones, crudely similar to the methods of Chinese lapidaries. The Provincial Museum at Victoria, B.C., has an exhibit illustrating such sawing of jade by the early B.C. Indians.

15. The fabulous CHI-LIN has the body of a deer, tail of an ox, scales of a fish, one horn covered with flesh to show that while prepared for war it desires peace. The Chi-lin does not tread on any living thing, even grass. The emblem of perfect goodness, it lives 10.000 years, it appears only when a virtuous sovereign is born or a good new government is started.

16. Most snuff bottles were obviously designed for presentations, the designs expressing best wishes for a long life (the SHOU sign, peach, crane, fungus, butterfly): for many children (pomegranate, grasshopper, gourd); for prosperity (goat, carp); or for happiness (Buddha's hand citron; et cetera Some made for birthdays include the recipients age in the design, such as forty eight SHOU signs, immortality; or it may be a hundred as a hope that he may live that long.

LOTUS, PURITY

17. Berthold Laufer identifies ROCK CRYSTAL bottles as "Canton glass" but this appears doubtful. Their cold feel shows the high heat conductivity of quartz; they pass ultra violet light like quartz; are harder than most glass; are entirely free of bubbles; and the interiors are obviously so shaped as to facilitate hollowing by lapidary methods. The Smithsonian Institution has a flawless sphere 12⅞" diameter of rock crystal from Burma.

18. Besides nephrite and jadeite a third mineral similar to jadeite and called CHLOROMELANITE, opaque green and black, is found in Chinese jade carvings, including the ancient.

19. Data on HO-SHÊN and CHIA CH'ING on Pages 1-3 is from official records reported in "A Manchu Monarch" by A.E. Grantham, see Bibliography.

20. LONG ELIZAS are ladies painted on Chinese porcelain, so called for the last 300 years from the name given them by the early Dutch importers, "lange liszen", which means "long stupids".

21. Turquoise is revered in Tibet as jade is in China, and has as many uses. The Tibetan name is GYU, pronounced "Yu", quite like the Chinese name for jade.

Turquoise is little known in China. That carved in Pekin came from Mongolia; that from Tibet was carved in Si-ngan Fu. The bottle on Page 20 is apparently Tibetan turquoise.

CARP, PROFITS

PRONUNCIATION OF CHINESE WORDS AS USUALLY SPELLED

a = father	ia = yarn	ch = jerk
ai = aisle	ie = siesta	ch' = chirp
ao = loud	ieh = yeh	k = go
e = bet	iu = adieu	k' = king
ê = err	j = how	p = back
eh = say	o = or	p' = pack
ei = feint	ou = owe	t = dab
en = men	u = flute	t' = tab
ên = fun	ü = her	hs = hush
erh = err	uai = wight	chih = chirp
i = machine	uei = weight	tzu = adze

YÜ = yer

FEI-TSUI = fay zuee

SHOU = show

HAN = hon

FÊNG HUANG = ferng whong

CH'I-LIN = cheeleen

MA SHAO SÜAN = ma show seran

CHENG WANG CHANG = jeng wong jong

REIGNS

1644-61	SHUN CHIH = shoon cher
1662-1722	K'ANG HSI = kong she
1723-35	YUNG CHÊNG, yoong jerng
1736-95	CH'IEN LUNG = chĕĕn loong
1796-1820	CHIA CH'ING, jeeah cheeng
1821-50	TAO KUANG = taow kuang
1851-61	HSIEN FÊNG = sheen ferng
1862-74	T'UNG CHIH = toong cher
1875-1908	KUANG HSU = guong shoe
1908-12	HSUAN T'UNG = shuan toong
1913-14	HUNG HSIEN, hoong shĕĕn

CYCLICAL DATES:

STEMS: CHIA = jaw; I = ee; PING; TING; MOU = mōw; CHI = jy; KING = geng; HSIN = sheen; YÊN = vun; KUEI = kay;

BRANCHES: TZÜ = dzer; CH'OU = chō; YIN; MAO = ma-owe; CH'EN = chen; SZÜ = zer; WU = woo; WEI = way; SHÊN = shern; YU = yoo; HSU = shoe; HAI = high.

DATE MARKS

As found on some Snuff Bottles, porcelain & others. (Dates are not always authentic)

CH'ING (MANCHU) DYNASTY 1644-1912

KHANG 光 大 GREAT

PERIOD 年 清 CH'ING

MADE 製 道 TAO

SCRIPT

PERIOD MADE TAO GREAT CH'ING KUANG ← usually omitted

SEAL FORM

治 GREAT

PERIOD CH'ING

MADE 順

REIGN OF

Shun Chih (1644-61)

PERIOD MADE

熙

康

Kang Hsi (1662-1722)

SEE NOTE 13

正

雍

Yung Chêng (1723-35)

隆

乾

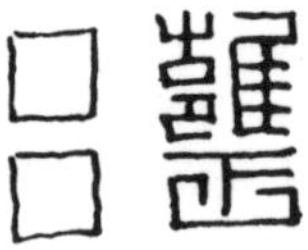

Ch'ien Lung (1736-95)

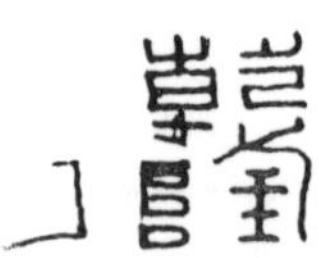

MOST OF THE FINEST BOTTLES WERE MADE IN CH'IEN LUNG REIGN.

Script date marks are also condensed to four characters, GREAT CH'ING omitted, as shown ↙

Script	Reign of	Seal
嘉 [PERIOD] 慶 [MADE]	Chia Ch'ing (1796-1820)	嘉 [PERIOD] 慶 [MADE]
道 光 [MADE] [PERIOD] [CH'ING] [GREAT]	Tao Kuang (1821-50)	道 光 [PERIOD] [MADE] [GREAT] [CH'ING] ↑ sometimes
咸 豐 □ □	Hsien Fêng (1851-61)	咸 豐 □ □
同 治 □ □	Túng Chih (1862-74)	同 治 □ □
光 緒 □ □	Kuang Hsu (1875-1908)	光 緒 □ □
宣 統 □ □	Hsuan Túng (1908-1912)	洪 憲 Hung Hsien (1913-14)

中華民國 REPUBLIC OF CHINA.

CYCLICAL DATES

Chinese porcelain and other objects, including a very few snuff bottles, are at times dated in cycles of 60 years starting from 2637 B.C.; we are now in the 77th cycle. One has to use other evidence as to what cycle any date belongs. Cyclical dates combine two characters, a "stem" followed by a "branch," as shown below:

TEN STEMS:

甲	乙	丙	丁	戊	己	庚	辛	壬	癸
CHIA	I	PING	TING	MOU	CHI	KENG	HSIN	VÊN	KUEI
							↓	↓	↓

TWELVE BRANCHES:

1	2	3	4	5	6	7	8	9	10
子	丑	寅	卯	辰	巳	午	未	申	酉
TZÜ	CH'OU	YIN	MAO	CH'EN	SZÜ	WU	WEI	SHÊN	YU
11	12	13	14	15	16	17	18	19	20
戌	亥	↖	↖ SEE	ABOVE		↖			
HSU	HAI	TZÜ	CH'OU	YIN	MAO	CH'EN	SZÜ	WU	WEI
21	22	23	24	25	26	27	28	29	30
SHÊN	YU	HSU	HAI	TZÜ	CH'OU	YIN	MAO	CH'EN	SZÜ
31	32	33	34	35	36	37	38	39	40
WU	WEI	SHÊN	YU	HSU	HAI	TZÜ	CH'OU	YIN	MAO
41	42	43	44	45	46	47	48	49	50
CH'EN	SZÜ	WU	WEI	SHÊN	YU	HSU	HAI	TZÜ	CH'OU
51	52	53	54	55	56	57	58	59	60
YIN	MAO	CH'EN	SZÜ	WU	WEI	SHÊN	YU	HSU	HAI

Recent cycles ended 1623, 1683, 1743, 1803, 1863, 1923.

Thus 1943 is 1943-1923 = 20th Yr., or KUEI WEI 癸未

The Cyclical date is often followed by the season, or number of the moon, 3rd Moon 三月 or may be combined with the Reign name.

RHYTICEROS PLICATUS

TYPES

This Edition has shown sketches of 61 snuff bottles made of twenty different materials in 34 general types. In order to make it a comprehensive collection of types it is hoped it will eventually include some of the following found in other collections but not yet acquired for this one in satisfactory specimens:

MATERIALS:

Chicken bone jade. See Page 17.
Jade with enamel inlay.
Agate, painted inside.
Lapis lazuli, dark ultramarine.
Aquamarine, light blue, not quartz.
Heliotrope or bloodstone, green, red spots.
Malachite; Jasper; Soapstone.
Coral; Iron; gold; Silver.
Gold Amber, fiery red and black
Hornbill beak, crimson and yellow.
Mother of pearl inlay in lacquer.
Porcelain, Sang-de-boeuf, and flambe.

SHAPES AND MOTIFS:

Buddha's Hand, See Page 31.
Ch'i-Lin, See Note 15.
Wicker ware shape.
Eight stallions of Mu Wang.
Lions playing ball.
Squirrels stealing grapes.
Liu Hai and his toad.
and many other legendary subjects.

BIBLIOGRAPHY

This is apparently the first book about Chinese Snuff Bottles. Below is listed material about them in other publications, in order of its value to the collector for reference:-

1. Tobacco and its Use in Asia, BERTHOLD LAUFER, Field Museum of Natural History, Anthropology Leaflet 18. 1924. 25¢. (Now Chicago Natural History Museum)
P. 32-39. 2700 words. Photogravures 15 bottles + 10 saucers.

2. Catalogue of a Collection of Ancient Chinese Snuff Bottles in possession of Mrs. George T. Smith, Chicago, by BERTHOLD LAUFER. Privately printed 1913 (Out of print)
63 pages. Detailed descriptions of 471 bottles.

3.A Snuff Bottles, ANN WENTWORTH. The Magazine Antiques, November, 1942. See 3B ↓
1600 words. Photos 31 bottles. Collection Albert M. Pyke.

4. Chinese Pottery & Porcelain, R.L. HOBSON. 2 volumes, Cassell & Co., Ltd., London.
Vol. 2, P. 202, 262-3, 266. 250 words. Photos Pl. 134, 5 bottles.

5. Chinese Art, S.W. BUSHELL, C.M.G., 2 volumes, Victoria & Albert Museum, London, 1924.
Vol. 2, Pages 41, 64, 66. 150 words. Photos 12 bottles.

6. The Story of Snuff and Snuff Boxes, MATTOON M. CURTIS, Liveright Publishing Corporation, 1935, $3.50.
Pages 93-98. 1300 words (inaccurate). Photos 29 bottles.

7. Jade Lore, JOHN GOETTE, Regnal & Hitchcock (Printed in Shanghai) Page 211, 130 words. Photos 6 bottles.

8. Chinese Jade Throughout the Ages, STANLEY CHARLES NOTT, B.T. Batsford, Ltd. London, 1936, $15.00
Page 142, 250 words. Color plate 6 bottles

9. Handbook of the Pottery & Porcelain of the Far East, R.L. HOBSON, C.B, British Museum, London, 1937, $1.50
Pages 112-113. 750 words. Photos 2 bottles.

10. Chinese Porcelain, Periods of K'ang Hsi, Yung Chêng, and Ch'ien Lung. The Victoria & Albert Museum, London, 1927, 1.50. Page 60 200 words. Photos 5 bottles.

11. Handbook of the Benjamin Altman Collection. The Metropolitan Museum of Art, New York City, 1928 Pages 16-17 300 words.

THE METROPOLITAN MUSEUM OF ART, N.Y.C., has for sale fine photographs of several hundred snuff bottles at 10¢ each.

12. A Manchu Monarch, A.E. GRANTHAM. George Allen & Unwin, Ltd., London. Page 56 reports Ho-shen's 2390 snuff bottles, 1801.

13. Lock, Stock and Barrel, DOUGLAS & ELIZABETH RIGBY. 1944, $5. rag paper $15. 570 fascinating pages about all sorts of collectors, ancient and modern, but not one word about snuff bottles!

14. Agate, OLIVER C. FARRINGTON, Field Museum of Natural History, Geology Leaflet 8, 1927., 50¢. Page 34, 120 words. (Now Chicago Natural History Museum)

15. Ivory in China, BERTHOLD LAUFER, Field Museum of Natural History, Anthropology Leaflet 21, 1925, 75¢. Page 68, 10 words. (Now Chicago Natural History Museum)

16. Nature in Chinese Art, ARTHUR DE CARLE SOWERBY. The John Day Co., 1940. $3.75. Pages 116-117. Photos 2 bottles.

17. Chinese Jade, STANLEY CHARLES NOTT. Record Press, Inc., St. Augustine, Florida, 1942, $.75 Page 384, 10 words.

38. Antiques as Decoration, EDWARD WENHAM, Arts & Decoration Magazine, Dec. 1928. Shows collection of Col. James A. Blair, Jr. 1200 words. Photos 18 bottles and the Collection in wall cases.

18. Loot of the Imperial Summer Palace at Pekin (By French and English armies, Oct. 7-8, 1860) Annual Report SMITHSONIAN INSTITUTION 1899-1900, Pages 601-635. This and the similar looting in June, 1900 of all the Pekin palaces by the armies of England, France, Russia, Germany, Japan, U.S.A., Italy, & Austria, at the end of the Boxer war, are the sources of many of the fine snuff bottles in our collections.

ADDITIONAL BIBLIOGRAPHY. Can you report further Chinese Snuff Bottle references. ?

4B. History of Ceramic Art in China, ALFRED E. HIPPISLEY, Smithsonian Institution 1902, also in the Report for 1900. 47 bottles described, none pictured.

5B. A Tempest in a Snuff Bottle, ELIZABETH RIEFSTAHL, The Brooklyn Museum Quarterly, April, 1938. 4000 words, pictures 9 bottles. See our Page 73.

5C Pottery & Porcelain of all Times and Nations, WM. C. PRIME, Harper Bros. 1878 900 words, 8 pictures on Chinese snuff bottles found in Egyptian tombs. Now superceded by RIEFSTAHL monograph above.

11 B. Handbook of Decorative Arts & Sculpture, THE MINNEAPOLIS INSTITUTE OF ARTS, 50cts, "The Searle Collection" 800 words, pictures 8 bottles. Also see Bulletin, Mch. 4, 1933, 800 words, 2 bottles

14B The Collectors First Handbook on Antique Chinese Ceramics, ELSE S DUNCAN, 1942, 70 words.

17B. Chinese Ceramics, Marquet de Vasselot, and Ballot, THE LOUVRE MUSEUM. Vol. 2, Plate 42, 4 bottles.

2A. Chinese Snuff Bottles, MARCUS B HUISH, London, 1895, is the ONLY KNOWN BOOK IN ENGLISH on the subject other than ours Privately printed, 149 copies, two known copies in U.S., Metropolitan Museum of Art, and Library of Congress (not loaned) 9000 words, 13 plates, 12 bottles pictured No new data in book.

2B Bibliotheca Nicotiana, 1880 catalog of Tobacco museum of WM. BRAGGE, Master Cutler of Sheffield, England. Includes a bare list of 628 bottles, no pictures Interesting listing of 150 snuff bottles not Chinese. Rare but can be borrowed from the Library of Congress by your library.

19. PI-YEN TS'UNG-K'O, all Chinese book on Snuff (Nose-tobacco) including bottles, 1870. Probably full of valuable data but is written in old literary Chinese very hard to translate. Can be borrowed from the Library of Congress.

The following articles on KU-YÜEH HSÜAN porcelain illustrate snuff bottles:

ANTIQUES, Oct. 1937, 2 bottles

INTERNATIONAL STUDIO, Dec. 1919 Page LXVI. 2 bottles.

BURLINGTON MAGAZINE, Dec. 1935, 11 bottles.

SMITHSONIAN INSTITUTION, Report for 1900, Pls. 18+19, lists # 323 is a snuff bottle.

ERRATA

Wrong bird on Page 105. It should be the Helmeted Hornbill (Rhinoflex vigil). of Sumatra. Bottle on P. 51B is a vertical slice thru the front of the "crane crest"

The bottle shown as brown nephrite on P. 16 and the Frontispiece is not jade at all, but some form of agate. (Pages 16 & 17 will be replaced in late books and Pages 51A, 51B, 107A, & 107B added)

Page 101. K'ANG HSI is pronounced "Kong She" not "Shy". (Corrected in books after Serial No. 100)

Page 53. Amber also came from YUNNAN PROVINCE in China, near Burma.

Page 75, start of last paragraph. There are twenty or more designs of these bottles, far more than six as stated in books earlier than #100.

Page 9 after line 11. "A portion of snuff is laid on the left hand, at the lower joint of the thumb, and thus lifted to the nose." Sir John Francis Davis, THE CHINESE, London, 1836. Other accounts say the palm of the hand.

INDEX

653 REFERENCES.

SUPPLEMENT

煙瓶

PI- YEN PING

← "SNUFF BOTTLE" in Chinese. "BĪYĔN PĪNG". Literally "Nose-tobacco bottle."

THESE ANALECTA are fragments of information gleaned from your letters, and libraries, to supplement the book OLD CHINESE SNUFF BOTTLES. This initial number will be distributed without charge. It is hoped that it will inspire many newsy letters that lead to new data. Our whole aim is maximum help to every snuff bottle collector. Will you help? Write!

Ex Prime Minister Churchill uses snuff from "a little antique silver box". (LEND-LEASE, Stettinius, P. 242) Add a note at top of Page 9, your copy of O.C.S.B.

Fruit on Page 11 is egg plant, the dark "Han" discoloration very aptly used for the ripe fruit, green jade for immature fruit and foliage.

The carving of rock crystal in China was promoted by Emperor Ch'ien Lung in 1775-96. Note 17, P. 100.

Data on the fine porcelain bottle shown on P. 61 is especially desired. The signature, CHUNG LUM, is a very rare feature on 18th Cent. Chinese porcelain.

Page 98, Note 14. A very full account of prehistoric jade implements in British Columbia and Alaska, with color plates, is #35 of Indian Notes & Monographs, Museum of the American Indian, Heye Foundation, N.Y.C.

Page 10, lines 4-8. Prescott says chalchivitl (jade) was of highest value among Aztec treasures.

古仿清大 "Great Ching, but after the ancient style."

An ivory bottle with microscopic inscription like that on Page 56 is dated 1939, made by "Old Swallow" of Nanking. Wonderful but modern.

The War is over, now it can be told. Our unique grass cloth bindings are from wall paper made in exotic variety years ago by Davidge & Company of Toronto, Canada, in a factory in Tokyo.

We have used small remnants found in Seattle, Vancouver, B.C., and Toronto, over a dozen interesting varieties, and need more. Can you help?

KU-YÜEH HSÜAN, or "Ancient Moon Pavilion" bottles, introduced to our book on Page 51A, are a deep subject. Later we will share our research with you. Meanwhile information will be welcome on any bottles you have, or know of, signed:

軒月古 OR 軒月古 or other variations.

LAUGHS? Two great libraries each thought our thin brochure was the whole book, kept it, wrote they would remit $12! A gentleman called on long distance phone to ask where he could buy printer's type like that used in the book, which is all hand lettered. We felt delightfully complimented.

Socks for babies are ideal for carrying snuff bottles; CADIE treated Furniture Cloth for polishing them; and DUPONT'S Household Cement for repairing spoons, stoppers, and stands.

Sales of our book all over the world to dozens of art museums, libraries, and universities, to the British Museum, are thrilling, very. But it is COLLECTORS it is made for and we want to reach first; do reply to our appeal to you on the back cover!

MADE OF ROCK CRYSTAL WITH MATRIX COLOR SMOKY

WORKMANSHIP VERY FINE SIZE, mm 65+9x30x27 (4)

PROBABLE REIGN CH'IEN LUNG DATES 1736-1795 (Note 1)

HAS ORIGINAL (2) SPOON-STOPPER OF ROSE QUARTZ ON IVORY VERDIGRIS

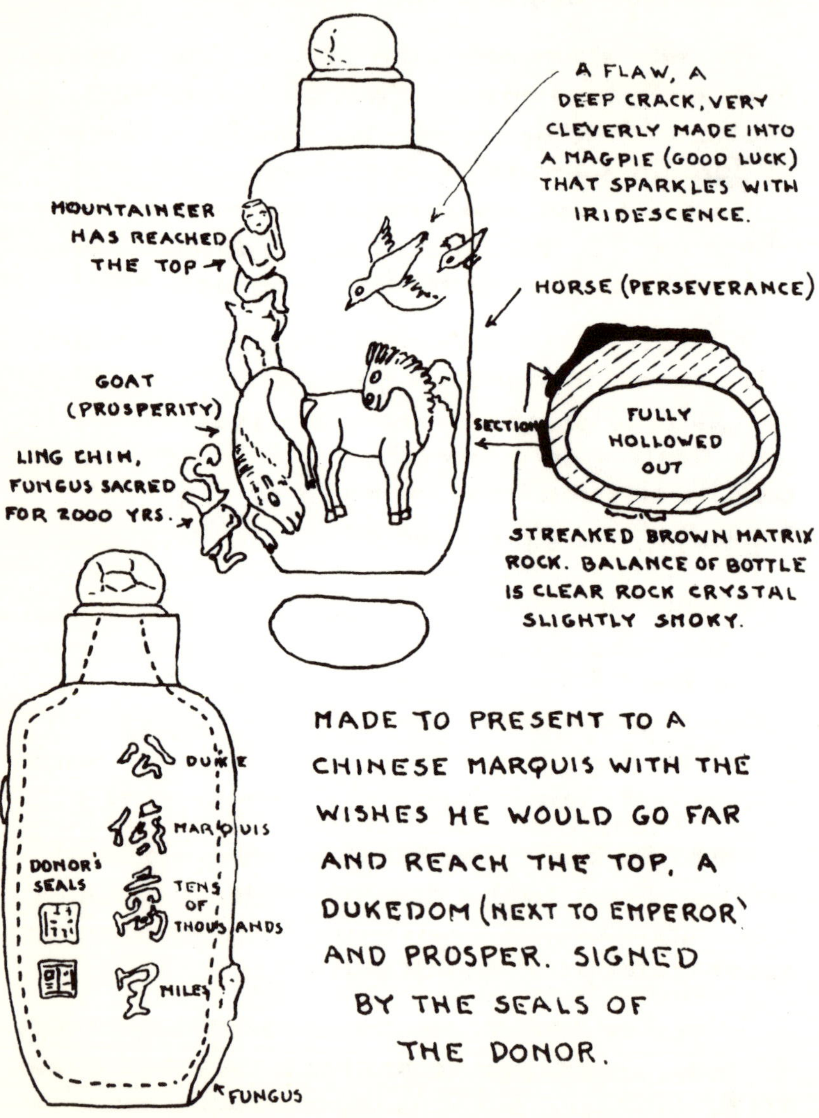

MADE TO PRESENT TO A CHINESE MARQUIS WITH THE WISHES HE WOULD GO FAR AND REACH THE TOP, A DUKEDOM (NEXT TO EMPEROR) AND PROSPER. SIGNED BY THE SEALS OF THE DONOR.

ACQUIRED FROM ARTHUR LOVELESS 2-1-46
ALPA

IN COLLECTION OF HENRY C. HITT

MADE OF ROCK CRYSTAL PAINTED INSIDE **COLOR** CLEAR

WORKMANSHIP MARVELOUS. BY MA SHAO-SÜAN **SIZE, mm** 55 + 7 x 30 x 16 (4)

PROBABLE REIGN TAO KUANG **DATES** SUMMER 1840 (Note 1)

HAS ORIGINAL (2) **SPOON-STOPPER OF** CORAL & BLACK HORN

HALF OF A CORAL MANDARIN CHAIN BEAD

BLACK HORN

ACTUAL SIZE (3)

MA SHAO-SUAN

IN PEKIN WRITTEN

FREE TRANSLATION OF INSCRIPTION

KENG TZŬ: SUMMER DAY
37= 1840

PAINTED STRING OF GOLD CASH STILL BRIGHT AFTER OVER 100 YEARS!

"BAREFOOTED AT THAT TIME MY THOUGHTS AIMLESSLY WANDERED OVER 10 CONTINENTS AND 3 ISLANDS FROM A PLACE OF PEACE ISOLATED FROM ALL CIVILIZATION WHERE GOLDEN BUTTERFLIES OFTEN MET AS FARIES."

LIU HAI, LEGENDARY BOY WITH IMMORTALITY WHO PERFORMED MIRACLES, PLAYING WITH HIS FAMOUS THREE LEGGED FROG. THE STRING OF CASH SHOWS HE WAS THE PATRON OF BUSINESS.

ACQUIRED FROM H. SOOYSMITH 7-18-46

STOO

116

MADE OF PORCELAIN COLOR WHITE

WORKMANSHIP MISSHAPEN SIZE, mm 49+5x39x15 (4)

PROBABLE REIGN TAO KUANG DATES 1821-1850 (Note 1)

HAS ORIGINAL (2) SPOON-STOPPER OF GOLDSTONE & BLACK HORN

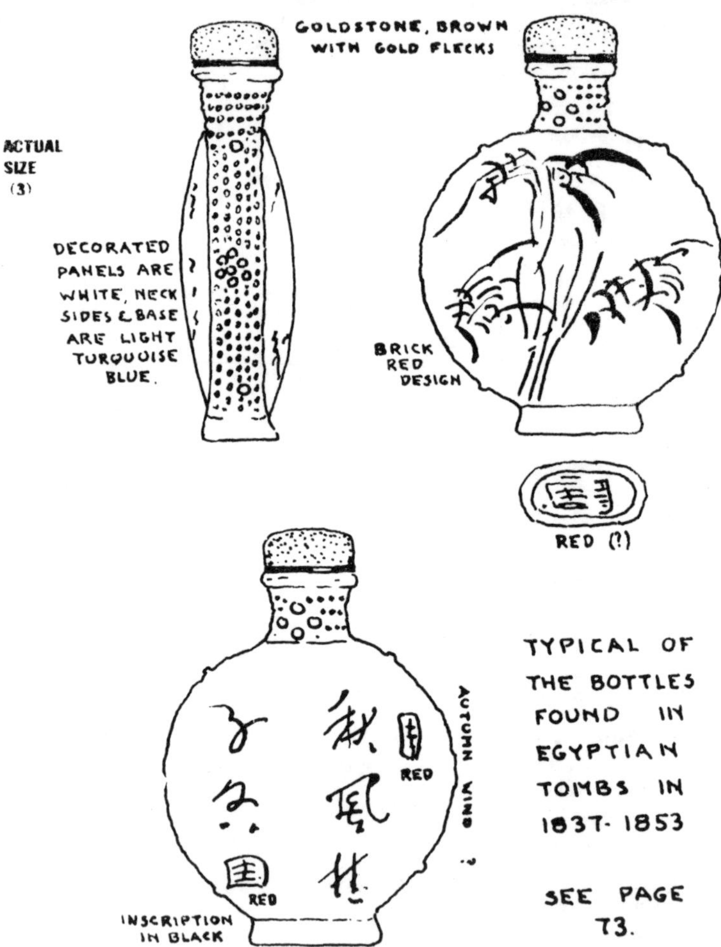

TYPICAL OF THE BOTTLES FOUND IN EGYPTIAN TOMBS IN 1837-1853

SEE PAGE 73.

FRAGRANCE OF THIS CERTAIN TREE COMES WITH AUTUMN WINDS.

ACQUIRED FROM H. SOOYSMITH 3-20-46

ABIE

IN COLLECTION OF HENRY C. HITT

MADE OF PORCELAIN, FÊNG TING **COLOR** CREAM

WORKMANSHIP FINE, MOLDED & INCISED **SIZE, mm** 47+6×21×17 **(4)**

PROBABLE REIGN CH'IEN LUNG **DATES** 1735-1796 **(Note 1)**

HAS ORIGINAL (2) SPOON-STOPPER OF CORAL

SHINY BLACK EYES WITH RIM BROWNISH UNGLAZED BODY, ALL ELSE CREAMY THICK GLAZE, FAINT CRACKLE.

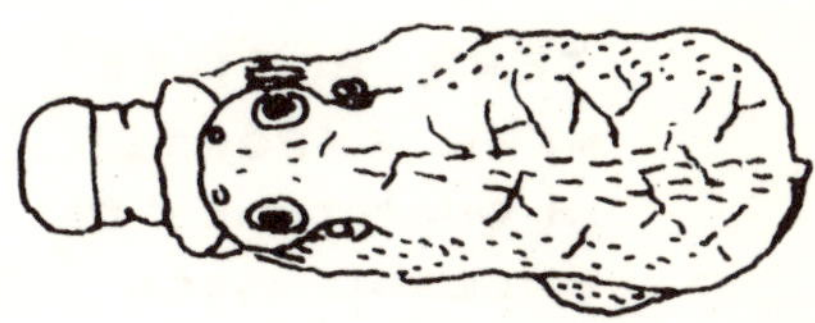

ACTUAL SIZE (3)

CHINESE BADGER, YEH MAO, "WILD CAT", REPUTED TO BE ABLE TO TRANSFORM INTO A MAN. RARELY USED IN DESIGN AFTER THE SUNG PERIOD, A.D. 1279.

TING WARE ORIGINATED IN TING CHOW IN THE T'ANG DYNASTY, A.D. 618-906, WAS PERFECTED UNDER THE SUNG EMPERORS, 960-1279, AND REVIVED AT CHING TE CHEN UNDER CH'IEN LUNG. THIS BOTTLE IS FÊNG, OR FLOUR TING. THE BODY, NOT QUITE A TRUE PORCELAIN, IS OFTEN CARVED OR MOLDED. THIS IS BOTH.

ACQUIRED FROM H. SOOYSMITH 3-21-46
SUCH

MADE OF PORCELAIN, UNDERGLAZE BLUE COLOR WHITE
WORKMANSHIP SUPERB SIZE, mm 46 × 27 DIA. (4)
PROBABLE REIGN K'ANG HSI DATES 1662-1722 (Note 1)
HAS ORIGINAL (2) SPOON-STOPPER OF NONE. IS A "TEAR BOTTLE".

ACTUAL SIZE (3)

"TEAR BOTTLES" WERE EXPORTED IN QUANTITIES TO HOLLAND, CIRCA 1700.

THE NAME IS OBSCURE, GIVEN BY EUROPEANS.

WITH STOPPERS ADDED THEY ARE SNUFF BOTTLES.

THIS IS THE BEAUTIFUL COBALT BLUE OF THE K'ANG HSI POTTERS, NOT THE "MOHAMMEDAN" VIOLET BLUE OF 100 YEARS EARLIER.

ACQUIRED FROM MRS. CLARK'S TREASURES, VANCOUVER, B.C. 10-18-45
INFI

IN COLLECTION OF HENRY C. HITT

MADE OF PORCELAIN, CARVED

COLOR PURE WHITE

WORKMANSHIP SUPERB

SIZE, mm 73+9 x 40 x 19 (4)

PROBABLE REIGN CH'IEN LUNG

DATES 1735-1796 (Note 1)

HAS ORIGINAL (2) SPOON-STOPPER OF GREEN GLASS

ACTUAL SIZE (3)

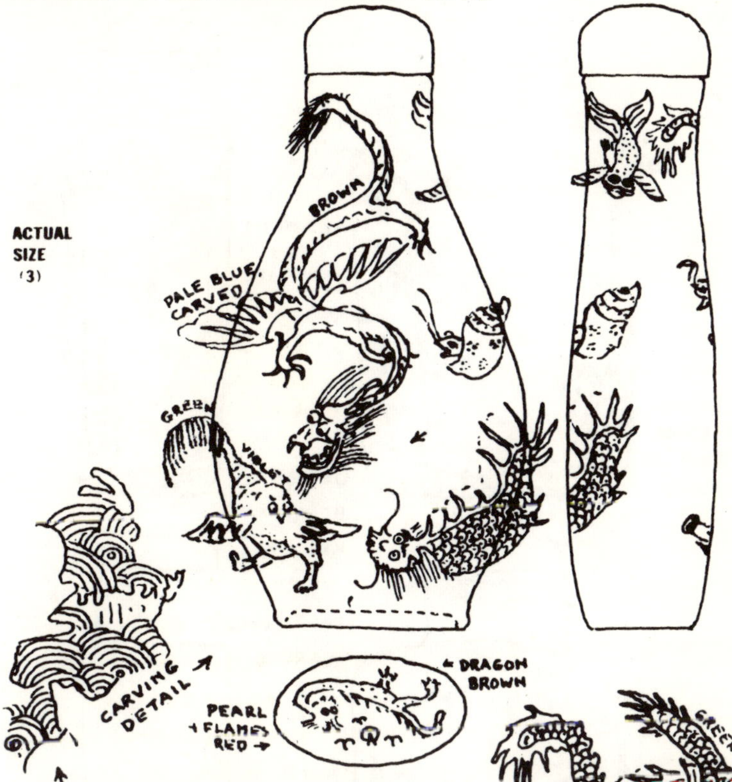

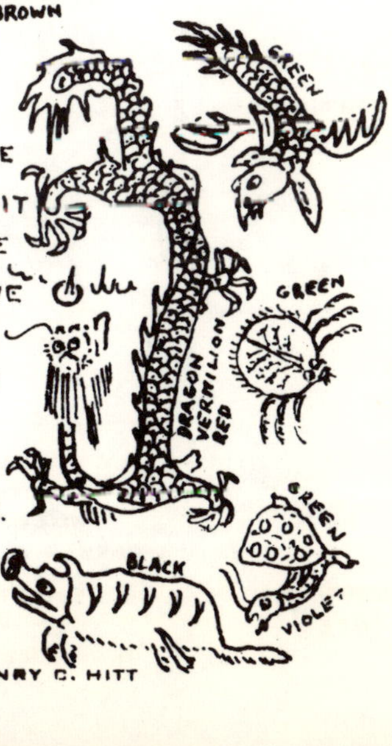

SPACES BETWEEN MONSTERS ARE PURE WHITE PORCELAIN, THE BISCUIT CARVED ALL OVER BETWEEN THE DESIGNS WITH AN INTRICATE WAVE PATTERN. WINGS & OTHER PARTS ARE ALSO CARVED. ALL DESIGN EXCEPT RED IS COVERED WITH CLEAR GLAZE, RED IS GLOSSY.

DRAGON ON BOTTOM OVER GLAZE.

ACQUIRED FROM MR. ARTHUR LOVELESS
AERX 11-24-45

IN COLLECTION OF HENRY C. HITT

MADE OF JASPER — COLOR BUTTERSCOTCH

WORKMANSHIP SUPERB — SIZE, mm 6+57 x 39 x 19 (4)

PROBABLE REIGN CH'IEN LUNG — DATES 1735-96 (Note 1)

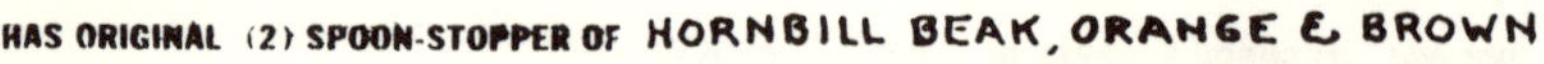

HAS ORIGINAL (2) SPOON-STOPPER OF HORNBILL BEAK, ORANGE & BROWN

BUTTERFLY, AN ANCESTOR

B

ACTUAL SIZE (3)

BAMBOO FOR LONG LIFE

HOLLOWING OF INTERIOR IS UNUSUALLY COMPLETE.

DESIGN IS IN LOW RELIEF VERY BEAUTIFULLY CARVED.

B

SEE FRONTIS-PIECE.

LOTUS FOR PURITY

A

VERY UNIFORM RICH BUTTERSCOTH BROWN SLIGHTY ← DARKER to LIGHTER →

"A" AND "B" SMALL DARK SPOTS WORKED INTO THE DESIGN

ACQUIRED FROM 4 SOOYSMITH 1-9-44 ATEX

IN COLLECTION OF HENRY C. HITT

MADE OF "CHICKEN-BONE" JADE COLOR CREAM

WORKMANSHIP FINE, VERY NICE SHAPE SIZE, mm 4+47 x 29 DIA.(4)

PROBABLE REIGN CH'IEN LUNG OR EARLIER DATES 1735-96 (Note 1)

HAS ORIGINAL (2) SPOON-STOPPER OF SILVER & JADE

ACTUAL SIZE (3)

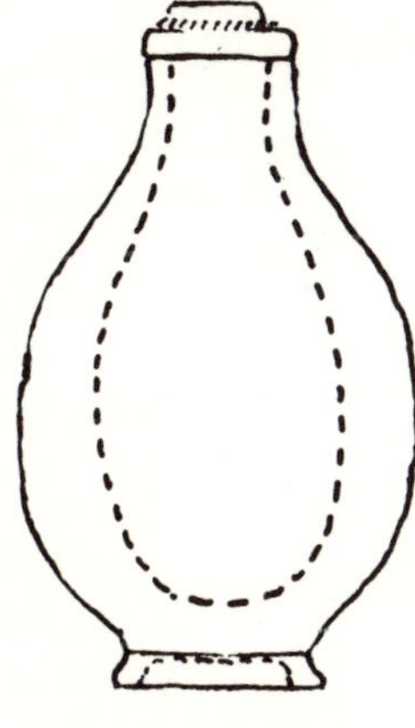

EMERALD GREEN JADE SET IN SILVER, SILVER SPOON.

BOTTLE CIRCULAR.

POSSIBLY WAS NOT ORIGINALLY A SNUFF BOTTLE. NECK LARGE, 7½ mm INSIDE DIA.

CHICKEN-BONE JADE IS USUALLY EXPLAINED AS BEING CALCINED OR BURNT JADE. IT IS ENTIRELY OPAQUE, CREAM COLOR AND THE SURFACE IS COVERED WITH A NETWORK OF VERY FINE CRACKS WHICH FILL WITH DIRT TO FORM HAIR NET PATTERN WHICH IF MAGNIFIED WOULD LOOK THUS:

IN COLLECTION OF H. SOOYSMITH